STRICTLY BIG BASS

Also by Joey Monteleone

I'll be Tennessean Ya'
His Story, Some Fish Tales and Tips

60 SEASONS
a fishing guide

STRICTLY
BIG BASS

Proven Trophy Tactics

JOEY MONTELEONE

WordCrafts

Published by WordCrafts Press
Cody, Wyoming 82414
www.wordcrafts.net

To my fathers, heavenly and earthly,
who have guided me on this joyous journey,
gave my dreams and wings,
and continue to inspire me.

Contents

Foreword

Catching "that trophy" big bass seems to be an ever-receding horizon. Well, that is for most of us. I know a guy who is an exception to that rule. A fisherman who has documented catches of well over a thousand of those green monsters weighing more than five pounds! He's a well-known professional who's not selling anything every five minutes on television. He's not promoting resorts or hiding his rods, reels, or lures when he's heading off the water at the end of the day!

There's a myriad of things that make him unique, but his non-self-serving desire to share how he accumulated such an incredible record is one of them. I've found his only motivation is the pure joy he feels witnessing or hearing about the success stories of anglers who have learned something from him.

One day over lunch we were discussing tournament strategies. After listening to my seemingly small pittance about getting a limit and then looking for that "kicker," he offered, "Not me, I'm going hunting that big girl right off the bat. And when I find her, I'm more likely to know where her sisters are hiding!" I was shocked, surprised really, and a thousand what, why, when and where questions followed over the course of the next several months. BIG bass expert angler Mr. Joey Monteleone gladly, openly answered every question I posed. I'd like to say those conversations were the catalyst for this, his latest offering, but that would be a lie. I will claim that it was anyway because I am a fisherman, and everyone knows fishermen lie. Those lies, of course, don't count on celestial scales. Utilizing some of the tips he shared with me, I bagged my two personal best bass that year, an eight pounder and a seven and a half. The thing is, both those fish were in areas I would never have fished at that time of year or with the lures I caught them with!

Last year I headed for a solo run to one of my favorite bodies of water. When I got to the ramp two very nice young men took pity on me and helped with my launch. In passing the one fellow said to me, "Don't waste your time throwing any cranks today. We been everywhere on this lake and haven't had a bite on one." After I pulled away from the dock I looked up at the front deck where one lonely rod with one very specific crankbait lay. Joey had recommended it the night before. Reluctant now, I pulled into the first cut and picked that rod up. On the third cast, a nice smallmouth hit it, then another. Every fish I caught that day (15) came on that Strike King 1.5 Oyster colored crankbait Joey recommended and predicted would work! I'm sure Joey has advised or mentored so many folks that this is just one of hundreds if not thousands similar success stories He has counseled me personally countless times.

So what? I'm 76 years at this writing. I've been fishing since I was nine years old when I started chasing that receding horizon. One would think I'd mastered the sport by now. I've read and reread his masterful first effort, *60 Seasons*, which was akin to having your own multi-species guide in the boat or on the bank with you. But *Strictly Big Bass* is a welcome, refreshing out-of-the-box approach to capturing lunker bass on a consistent basis. It contains tried and true approaches, many of which this old dog has never considered. Joey sums up his philosophy with this simple statement, "Most people want to find those five fish; I want to find five-pound fish!" He keeps a yearly journal wherein he documents each of over a thousand fish he catches each year. And now he adds to his personal knowledge having his excellent fisherwoman wife compete with him every day on the water. Debbie set a personal best last

season landing an eight-pound largemouth out of Woods reservoir in Tennessee. My guess is she probably got the jump on all of us reading the manuscript.

Conventional fishing catches conventional fish according to Joey. So *Strictly Big Bass* requires a different approach, some adjustments to strategy and tactics, and a willingness to set aside some old bad habits. Luckily, I have been the beneficiary of his friendship, wisdom, and mentorship. I know one can have fifty years of experience or they can have one year of experience fifty times. Take your talents and experience and do yourself a favor. Secure for yourself an additional sixty plus years of experience from one of the country's most successful professionals, Joey Monteleone!

We can't conclude this forward without a word about the man. He is a super patriot, a devout man of faith, a good husband and family man. He absolutely loves talking to people, so if you meet him at a book signing, personal appearance, in the local tackle shop at the ramp launching his red white and blue Jackson Kayak or in the supermarket, go introduce yourself to him. If you do you are in for a treat—and maybe a great tip!

~Michael Vines

I have been fortunate to have known Joey Monteleone—angler, communicator, and a wonderful friend—for many years. If I had a tackle box filled with blessings, he'd be in there.

In this book, *Strictly Big Bass,* my long time friend of over 40 years reveals things he's learned in a lifetime of catching trophy bass, things you probably never knew about America's number one game fish.

Strictly Big Bass should be on every angler's shelf! Read it! *Strictly Big Bass* is simply another masterpiece from one of the best fishermen in the world—a person I call "Brother Joey!

~Bill Dance

Humble Beginnings

Little fish are liars; big fish hold all the secrets.

Catching any fish is an accomplishment. We all heard it many times, *I just want to catch at least one.* It could be a kid on a creek bank or a seasoned angler in a high-powered bass boat, all in search of that elusive bass. It all begins with that silent prayer for some degree of success; fool that wonderfully wild creature into *taking the bait.* The journey can be with a cup of worms or an enormous collection of plastic boxes holding this season's can't miss artificial baits. Most of us can easily recall two fish—the first one and the biggest one. The trap we fall into is the goal of not getting *skunked,* zeroing and telling our fish story about the reasons they weren't biting that day or the painful tale about the one that got away. In our quest to catch fish, even the smallest bass give us that feeling of accomplishment—I did it! Unfortunately, this masks what every person truly wants—that monster fish that gives us bragging rights. With each cast we display that eternal optimism of *I'm going to set the hook on a giant.*

My goal with this book is not to help you catch a bunch of fish, it's to help you catch a bunch of BIG fish.

Little fish are like babies, always hungry and making mistakes because they lack experience of the world around them. Let's be honest a fish hitting any bait is making a mistake; it's a response to a stimulus provided by the person casting and retrieving (in most

1

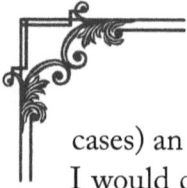

cases) an artificial bait. In this book you will repeatedly read what I would characterize as my theories—theories that are based off decades of experience with little scientific basis but have fooled the superior of the species, bass that would be considered trophy size. Let's quantify that, for a largemouth bass, the most pursued species on the planet, a ten-pounder is recognized as the yardstick of epic accomplishment, but a five-pound largemouth is a trophy. In the case of the less widely distributed smallmouth, a fish above five pounds is good, but that fish pushing the scale past that five-pound mark brings the admiration of your fellow fishermen.

As far as subspecies, spotted Kentucky bass of five pounds is cause for celebration. Keep in mind world record numbers as recognized by the governing bodies of such things range from the revered record of largemouth bass established in June of 1932 in a slough located in Georgia tilting the scales at 22 pounds 4 ounces with the smallmouth record a Dale Hollow Lake fish, shared by Tennessee and Kentucky, is a giant sitting at 11 pounds 14 ounces caught in 1955. The current record for spotted bass, a California fish weighing in at 11 pounds 4 ounces. You might note that in each of these species, in my opinion, catching a huge bass half the weight of any of the world record bass family should be considered a genuine trophy, but every fish caught is a victory and can be celebrated, it's one of the hallmarks of bass fishing—every catch provides a story.

The purpose of this book is to give the reader the benefit of my experience and success in cracking the code for what it takes to find and catch that fish of your dreams. The most dedicated bass casters recall every detail of two fish; their first and their biggest. The tactics between the covers of this book is meant to deliver the biggest bass of your life to your waiting grip.

In a treasured memory I was privileged to having this very discussion with the iconic and legendary Bill Dance, he relived the story of his own coveted first fish.

"My father and grandfather were both fishermen, my grandpa

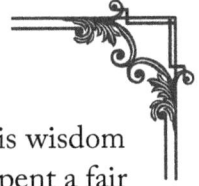

observed and studied the fish and often would share his wisdom with me. I got to tag along on many of their trips and spent a fair amount of time using antiquated tackle and live bait, catching black perch out of a local tiny Tennessee spot known as Mulberry Creek. Like many folks in our community I'd frequent the local country store that had a little of everything. One day I noticed a frog pattern bait in a display case and asked to inspect it a little closer. The store owner obliged, and I scanned every detail of the shiny new lure. 'That one costs 75 cents, Bill,' the owner said. I handed it back over to be returned to the display since I had no money.

"One day Grandpa was planning a fishing trip to Cumberland Springs, and I was going to be allowed to come along. Grandma was going also. She would find a shady spot and set out a quilt and crochet as we roamed the banks in search of fish. Grandma looked at me and said, "I think I know what you need," and unraveled a bandana revealing three shiny new quarters! A quick *thank you* and I was off to the store to get my own bait! Now my True Temper metal rod with an old Shakespeare reel had a real bait, an early Arbogast leopard frog pattern Jitterbug tied to it. After several false casts I threw my bait into the middle of a pool and watched as *two* bass approached it. I let sit, and when I slowly moved it, they followed the bait; rest and another short retrieve and the bigger of the two bass slammed my frog. Anxious to not let my fish get away I threw the whole rod and reel backward and started a hand over hand retrieve. I soon was racing toward Grandpa with my prize firmly clutched in my hands. 'That's a big Big Mouth,' Grandpa said. 'Let's put it on the stringer.'

"I wanted to put it in the car so it wouldn't get away. We weighed that fish on an old gadget called a *Fish DE-LIAR* and then secured my prize on an old metal clip stringer attached to a tree root. On the way home we stopped at a grocery store because thy had scales ,and my first largemouth bass weighed in at two pounds five ounces. That fish changed my life!"

My own story goes like this—as a young boy interested but

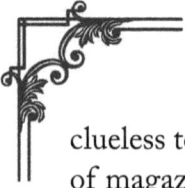

clueless to the world of bass fishing, I recall looking at the covers of magazines found in the racks of many stores. Occasionally, I also would pick up a Saturday morning fishing show on one of the four local TV channels we received. Armed with very little information and even less tackle I would take a walk to a small stream in Cedar Hill, Missouri, Skull Bone creek to see if I could fool anything swimming in the shallow water. I could see them, but I couldn't catch anything. I was oblivious to the fact that if I could see them, logically, they could see me. So, trip after trip—zero fish.

A late spring day found me walking toward a local pond, surrounded by a field of broom sage. I continued on a well-worn path where others had walked the banks ignoring the NO TRESS-PASSING sign. I had gained permission by performing a few farm duties for the owner. Briefly stopping to make one turn with a shovel in a spot along side a chicken coop to dig a few nightcrawler worms, I had my bait. Pulling a large night crawler worm from the coffee can, I carefully stitched the worm onto a small hook and adjusted my cork float to about ten inches above the hook. Walking to the base of a willow tree, I used a pendulum motion to guide my bait to the base of the weeping willow. Almost instantly the cork danced and disappeared, my reaction was to swing back and flop my first ever bass to my feet. Gathering my tackle more than my composure, I ran home to show off the fish, likely about a solid one pounder, that bass would forever change my life. That largemouth launched a life-long love affair with fishing and the never-ending search for that next BIG bass.

TROPHY TIP: In any way you can, check the surface water temperature before or after you launch to help determine the mood of the bass. While bass can be caught at just about any temperature, they are most active in the 60 to 75-degree range. A small pool thermometer or any number of electronics will do. This will also seasonally give you a hint as to the spawning mode of the bass or the rate of digestion.

2

Below The Surface, Basic Beliefs

Theories

All of our opinions and theories are often unsubstantiated beliefs, just educated guesses. My own theories come from analyzing an extensive amount of details from really bad days and the most memorable and productive trips. I journal, research, and add a dose of science where possible to build on those theories through the pregame planning before launch and throughout the trip. Any scientific testing has components like a standard environment (impossible in the outdoors) and continual testing until you reach repeatable, predictable results. On days when you catch nothing, don't consider those a failure—you actually still learn or reinforce something that you might have previously been exposed to and might again every single time your bait hits that water.

Bass behavior can be tricky because it depends on several factors. A self-imposed rule in bass fishing is to erase from your vocabulary and thinking two words; *never* and *always*. These do not exist in fishing. What you can have are frequently recognized similarities.

Catching Fish Isn't Hard, Finding Fish Is Hard

With the advent of most recent technology, electronic tools like Live Scope, Forward Facing Sonar, and Active Target images of fish appear in pixels on a screen along with lake bottom and cover—all are displayed, allowing the angler to present baits (also showing on

the screen) to the fish in the range of the transducer which sends the signal back to the unit. (Disclaimer: In my opinion the use of electronics has the potential to cause the user to be separated from their senses. In short don't abandon common sense and your inherent intuitive abilities by just staring at a screen.) I am in no way against the use of any kind of technology. What would fishing be like without the development of rods, reels, line, the trolling motor and so much more? On the plus side, a visual study of many game fish is the physical eye placement. Because of the way the eyes are oriented, it's desirable in many instances to have the bait slightly above the fish and in close proximity to the bass in order for it to look like it's easy to catch and minimal energy is needed to feed on it. Big fish don't get big by chasing food sources a long distance. Ask any crappie fisherman employing the new imaging technologies, and the most common response is place the bait within inches of the fish and just above it.

THEORY—In the business world, it's called return on investment, ROI. The shortest distance a fish moves to get the biggest, highly nutritional meal means that fish that grows the largest. It really makes sense.

Many people go into what I refer to as a "casting coma," cast after cast, no strikes, and then it becomes mindless casting not even expecting to get a bite. This proves to be disastrous when the moment of truth arrives unexpectedly. Once I enter an area I truly believe has BIG bass potential I do a few things:

1. I throw the quietest bait first. This is less likely to tip off a spooky fish, then move up in chronological sound progression from quietest to loudest. *Personal experience—many times while filming our TV show, *Tennessee's Wild Side*, I announced to the cameraman "roll on me" which was my way of saying, *I'm going to catch a fish right here.* First cast, *boom,* a bite, often a good size fish. After landing the bass

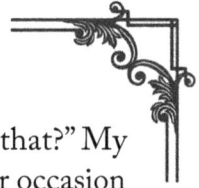

the cameraman would ask, "How did you know that?" My response was that I could just sense it. On another occasion filming on a small lake, I spotted a single stump along a small patch of lily pads, on a distinct point, and in eight feet of water. Again I gave my cameraman the verbal heads up and pitched a jig next to the stump and watched as my line immediately began to swim out toward deep water, a quick hook set and was soon lipping a seven-pound largemouth bass. Visually everything lined up for a fish to be there, the proper depth, then good cover, and previous experience just lead me to make a cast to the spot.

2. I always cast past the spot in which I believe the fish is staged. Casting directly on top of them can push them out, spook them, or give them additional time to view my lure. I want the bait to get into their line of sight for a minimal amount of time so they must decide quickly as to whether to take it or allow it to pass by. Especially when fishing topwater, this bit of advice is most valuable. The longer a bass is allowed to look at an artificial bait in the mid water depths or top water columns, the less likely it is to hit it. Baits on the bottom or swimming type lures are the exception. This is particularly important in throwing spinnerbaits and crankbaits and getting a deflection bite from the bass.

THEORY—Bass have relatively small brains, but while you're in recreational mode; they're in survival mode. The point being bass are not cognitive creatures—they react to external stimuli. My opinion is fish DO NOT learn, but they can become conditioned. Sight, sound, vibration, and other sensory clues can be noticed but can alarm or condition the fish to not strike. For this reason, I make a few casts and then move or switch baits or presentations. When you continually throw to a fish, it most likely knows something has entered their home area, if they don't hit after a couple of casts then you are conditioning the fish to not pay attention to the crankbait,

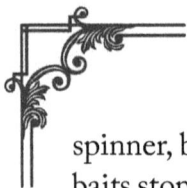

spinner, buzzer, or other offering. My belief is this is why certain baits stop working, rattling baits versus silent baits, wide wobbling crankbaits versus tight runners, large lures versus the downsized versions are all possible example and solutions.

Sound is one of the most misunderstood aspects of the underwater world of the bass by the bass fisherman. Years ago, the elderly fishing persons always advised people to be quiet or they would scare off the fish. While normal conversation does little to disrupt a bass, sharp or unnatural sounds will cause them to go into a negative mode. Sensing an intruder doesn't mean they will leave an area, but it's likely they will move into heavy cover or seek a closer position to an escape route, normally deeper water.

To put this into a more understandable science-based perspective, sound travels through water five times faster than it does through air! Sound can be a negative influence on game fish. Rattling type baits, crankbaits, lipless cranks, rattling spinners, and jigs equipped with rattles can be used in *dirty* water or around aggressive fish, but as a rule I use silent artificial lures. Tips I often gave at seminars were to tournament competitors who talked of fish being spooked when they entered areas that had previously gotten a high degree of fishing pressure. The answers were in three parts: shut down the big engine long before entering your fishing water, use the wind to drift you into position as much as possible, and if you're using a two-bladed propeller (the most common) on your trolling motor, change it to a three-bladed prop. The three blades not only sound different but actually create curiosity, drawing the attention of your target fish.

Where are they?

The search for bass is a puzzle with 500 pieces. Let's preface this by saying an attribute you should often apply using this theory, they don't all do the same thing at the same time. This theme will be repeated often in this book. Knowing your quarry and in dealing

with any wild creature there is a huge advantage to educating yourself as to their habits, likes, and dislikes. My choice to not use electronics does force me to be more aware of natural and visual clues, and any success I realize on a big fish bite automatically is committed to memory.

Getting the edge on bass

Fishing or hunting or just developing stalking outdoor skills will lead you to a few commonalities. One of my favorites is the use of edges. As a deer hunter, edges come into play often. Feeding areas, bedding spots, entering the woods or agricultural fields are very often used in paths that could be defined as edges. For bass, edges are an integral part of their feeding, ambush, migration, and other activities. Edges and their use are limited in the eyes of many anglers, they immediately think of the shoreline and leave it at that. Open up your imagination to the other possibilities, and it will make you a better angler. If you've been relegated to walking and fished from the bank of a creek or pond, how often have you had a fish at the last second hit your bait almost at your feet? Edge! They use the edge to trap any possible food source. Ever had that happen right at the side of your boat? Edge! When bass push a school of shad to the surface, gravity is their friend, the shad can jump but the bass is waiting to swallow as many as possible, and again the surface is an edge. Bass watch as your bait flutters down to the bottom and stare at it. You move it slightly, and the bass inhales the lure off the bottom—another edge. The side of a big submerged tree, a bridge piling, a wing dam—those and more are all edges. Work those edges!

TROPHY TIP: Be observant and watch for any movement that might tip you off to the presence of a fish. A disturbance around lily pads, through moss, a fish chasing bait; all of these are visual clues.

3

Focus On Their Four Needs

The BIG bass do things well to thrive; the others just survive. Things they have in common are basic bass needs. There are four basic needs. Find the area that serves all these needs and I guarantee you'll eventually find big bass.

- OXYGEN—Scientific studies show that for fish to do well they need dissolved oxygen at levels of between 5–6 parts per million. Low levels or less than 3 parts per million of dissolved oxygen threaten the survival of freshwater fish. As in humans, no oxygen, no breathing, no life. Dissolved oxygen in warm summertime waters is decreased and often leads to the phenomenon known as "die off" and the mishandling of fish whether from recreation or tournaments can also lead to high levels of mortality. Increased oxygen at times can draw and hold fish. Moving waters in the form of feeder creeks in lakes or even secondary creeks entering rivers or rivers themselves can be hot spots providing the much-needed oxygen at certain times.

- FOOD—Big bass are the most efficient predators. They are found in places that offer diverse forage bases and in large amounts. What they eat can determine their size, health, and life span. The diet of bass in studies shows large amounts of shad, and there's a logical explanation for this. Shad are often the most abundant food source. Given the opportunity

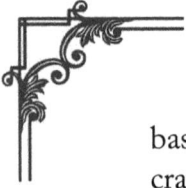

bass will seek out and suck up every available crawfish. If crawfish came with a nutritional label like our food, it would show highly desirable contents. I refer to crawfish as the "Red Bull" for bass—high energy and packs the pounds on. For very five pounds of crawfish eaten by a bass it gains a pound, nothing else comes close. One look at a largemouth bass tells the story; if they can catch it and it fits in their mouth, they'll eat it.

- COVER—In the case of the largemouth bass they are classically object-oriented. Drawn to various kinds of cover, the search can be maddening. Every body of water has something the largemouth bass can relate to, hide behind, use as an ambush point or as a resting spot. In a bowl-shaped lake bass will even go to single objects, one boulder rock, a single stump, a clump of aquatic water weeds, or any such attraction. This is where the most fundamental difference occurs with largemouth versus smallmouth bass. Smallmouth relate to deeper water and the contours or points contained there. The same stump that holds a largemouth bass means little or nothing to a smallmouth if there is deep water available.

- DEEP WATER CLOSE BY—For many species of freshwater fish this holds true, deep water for security and escape is essential. Often times when you hook a really big bass, it's been my experience they will do one of two things: try to "bury up" in heavy cover, or head to deep water. Smallmouths are notorious for this behavior. Deep water feels like a safe sanctuary to bass.

In recent public statements, two of the all-time best professional anglers admitted that they favor shallower water. Rick Clunn said, "I'm a shallow water fisherman. I stay in 15 feet of water or less," while Kevin VanDam shocked people by saying he focused on five feet of water for many of his tournament days! My records show similarities in that the vast majority of my BIG bass came from three to eight feet of water.

Once you locate places like this on your favorite fishing hole you will experience repeated results in consistently catching bass and most likely a big fish. In these places bass will become resident fish and only have to relocate if the food sources leave. Migrations from shallow water occur during the shad spawn and in the fall when giant schools of shad are necessary for the feeding binges prior to winter. When fish of any size are removed from these areas or die, another fish will move in. These places become legendary to guides, tournament fishermen, and others chasing the big bite.

Having found an area in a local large lake that served all the primary needs of a bass, I was filming a TV show under the title of *Wild Side Guide (Tennessee's Wild Side)* with a good friend. We were both in the bow of the boat, and I sensed that we were getting ready to catch a fish on camera. This spot had all the necessary components to consistently hold fish. There was adequate depth, a slopping bank going from two to ten feet of water, lots of rock to draw crawfish, and submerged wood with aquatic vegetation adjacent to the downed tree. We both saw a decent bass sitting in a small cut, but it slowly swam away as we approached. I backed the boat up and announced to my friend (and to the camera), "I can catch that fish." A quick pitch of a jig into the exact spot we had spotted the fish, a brief pause, and the bass swam back and took an inverted position staring at the crawfish imitating jig. "Watch this," I said and gave a slight twitch to the bait, and the bass instinctively inhaled it. That fish realized something had entered its area, could potentially be a food source, and merely reacted out of a normal instinct. The key for me that gave me the confidence was the fish moved off slowly and in a straight line. Observations like this and the applications of these in real life situations are the genuine highlights for me.

THEORY: My experience has led me to believe a fish that swims away on a straight line saw something it didn't like. A fish that swims out on a zig-zag pattern hears something and responds by

darting away as a defense mechanism because they cannot locate the intruder. That fish may return, but it would be much later and not be as catchable as the fish spooked by an unusual sight.

TROPHY TIP: Make a mental note to journal all the details of trophy catches after your trip. Once you become familiar with a body of water places that fit the four needs of a bass will become spots you hit each time and will cut your search time and likely increase your catches. Even if a BIG bass is removed or dies another will move into these honey holes.

4

CONVENTIONAL FISHING
CATCHES CONVENTIONAL FISH

The fishing media blitz that exists now creates a common mind-set. Racks of magazines, online posts, social media, pod casts, cable shows, personal appearances, and TV commercials blasted every seven minutes are all geared toward promoting *the catch*. The big-name pro, living legends, and the appeal of the fellow amateur angler all tout the *can't miss* bait now available in the store or from the online supplier. In bass fishing, like many other facets of life, there are the staples, gotta haves, go to baits, rods, reels, and accessories that are marketed as your ticket to success. The follow-the-leader mentality sends the message; *If that's what he/ she is using I need that and need it now*. Innovation is a great thing, basic approaches are also good, and certainly the baits, tackle, and techniques that fall into the "sexy" category are hard to resist. *It has to be true, I saw on TV, YouTube, Facebook Live or the internet!* You watch in awe as fish after fish comes to the grip of a superstar angler. But wait, where's the BIG fish?

Most organizations focus on catching numbers of fish. Other discussions center around catching 20 fish a day, five fish limits in tournaments, and exotic guided trips offering one hundred bass while you're on the magical waters.

There's nothing wrong with catching several fish, but the first few truly BIG bass you lip changes you forever. Initially it's, "I

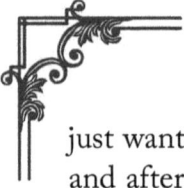

just want to catch a fish," then "I want to catch a bunch of bass," and after the first trophy, "I want to catch a bunch of BIG fish." Marketing or advertising doesn't portray the excited angler hauling in a 12-inch bass, it's always the spray coming off a true trophy. The unspoken message, *Want to catch the fish of your dreams, buy this, boat, this bait, come to this destination.*

We become educated to think like our idols do and take their advice as to what to fish, where to fish and when, and magically it works. BUT is that to catch a few fish or target the trophy size fish? I've often said most people want to catch five, and I want to catch A FIVE. The problem—when you swing for the fences you often strike out. My methods would be viewed by many as unconventional, and they're right, because "conventional fishing catches conventional fish."

I had a famous tournament angler once tell me if he caught a big fish most often it was by accident. A common tournament strategy has been to go catch a limit then try for a "kicker" (big) fish. When I fished tournaments, I went first to the spots that I thought positioned me to catch the biggest bass quickly, thinking I could catch and fill out my limit with the standard keeper-size afterwards. There's more of them, and the really good competitors might get to the large fish before me—even if some landed them accidentally. Using my unorthodox strategy earned me several big bass checks and I still placed high in many tournaments. Once, upon arrival to a tournament site to be held on a large river, I laughingly boasted that they could go ahead and write me the big bass check now. I felt my familiarity with river fishing and previous experience with BIG bass in rivers gave me an advantage. As predicted, I cashed that check.

The logic for me is many-faceted. In lakes that are highly pressured, many of the anglers have bought into the hype of what the bass are biting, and everyone has the lure of the week tied on and is peppering the banks with the identical bait. This is one of the reasons I often employ old proven lures and am a fan of altering baits as well as using custom colors.

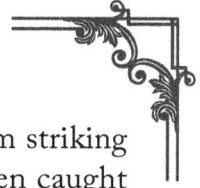

THEORY: Multiple exposures will dissuade fish from striking something they've seen repeatedly or even worse been caught on. In the fishing world we refer to this as becoming *lure shy*, and you can see it in display tanks and in store aquariums. Later we'll discuss why this doesn't happen as often with live bait.

Bass, being wild creatures, can become conditioned and learn to avoid danger (being caught) not to mention in your local lake the chances are high that a five-pounder has already been caught a half dozen times. In fishing discussions, often others will come to a consensus as to appropriate times to try various lures or techniques. For several seasons I fell for the hype and then eventually began thinking independently and NOT coincidentally began catching a few more big bass. A great example is the traditional viewpoint of when to break out the top water lures. I wanted to know how early in the year and at what water temperature bass would begin to blast surface baits. I would get quizzical looks and even lots of unrequested advice as to the logic of working surface lures at times. Many fishing folks would recommend not tossing top water lures until the surface temperatures were in the middle 60s. My view was if you catch five (or more) bass when you first start fishing the top you started too late. When did they first show interest in these lures? I discovered water temperatures around the 50-degree mark could produce hits on my top water lures! I also caught some of my biggest bass on minnow plugs, buzzbaits, prop baits, and cup faced poppers early in the year. I would have missed out on this if I had followed the conventional wisdom. Conventional fishing catches conventional fish.

I chuckled as I watched so-called experts advise people to use smaller blades on their spinnerbaits to match the size of the shad that had been hatched that year. In my opinion and my experience that's exactly backwards. Here's why, if you're competing with schools of shad that are an inch and half long and throwing a spinnerbait blade that's an inch a half long, it gets lost in a school of 500

hundred shad. I do just the opposite on a ⅜th ounce spinnerbait I remove the standard blade, likely a #4 ½, and replace it with a much larger #7 ½ blade. *You have to be careful to not overwhelm the bait and not make this adjustment with a lightweight lure. This blade displaces more water, gets more flash, and is highly visible to the bass seeking late year shad. Will you catch *more* fish with this tactic? Not likely. Will you catch BIGGER fish? It's more likely. Conventional fishing catches conventional fish.

When looking for a giant bite (I always am) while throwing a buzzbait, I go to the biggest blade I have in the box. The only time I change is in ultra-clear water and no wind. Working that bait around heavy cover and keeping it moving gives the fish less time to scrutinize it and increases your chances of drawing a hit from a heavyweight. Big sizes sometime intimidate anglers (and little fish), but BIG bass are looking for big meals. Your presentation has to be exact, but the return is worth it if you're on the prowl for a huge fish.

One aspect of my fishing success as a result of me guiding formally (being paid) or informally with family and friends is the transfer of knowledge to another angler. Whether fishing in a boat beside me or alongside of me I have guided several people to their biggest bass ever. Two of these people boated bass over nine pounds! Others have successfully landed an eight-pound largemouth, with several others catching bass in the five to seven pound category. Proof that the approach and presentations that I have used over the years work for others also.

One other detail I employ is showing the fish something different than almost anyone else. The use of out-of-production baits, altering baits, and the development of a new color each have paid off for me. Working with a lure manufacturer, MidSouth Tackle, I developed a silver soft plastic tube which became wildly popular. After a few seasons I asked to add a new look to the Monteleone silver tube—a bit of red glitter we called bloodshot—and it started catching crappie (which both were originally designed for), but

bluegill AND bass began to be regular catches on the same bait. With the success on the soft plastic, I reached out to friend and custom lure painter, Tony Evans (Evans Custom email bleudog25@ yahoo.com), and asked to recreate the color or hard baits, cranking plugs, lipless, and diving baits as well as minnow imitating lures. Lightning struck twice! The custom baits began fooling good bass immediately even on waters that were receiving a high degree of fishing pressure.

There are many more examples of thinking and applying unconventional tactics. You have to decide if you're going with the crowd or are willing to break out of the pack and set your sights on the monsters in your home waters.

TROPHY TIP: In the search for BIG topwater bass, sometimes they'll hit and miss the surface bait, very often a quick cast of a Texas-rigged soft plastic lure, to the same fish, or same area will produce a strike. You've gotten the fish's attention and the next thing in will draw strikes many times. Have a rod rigged and ready to cast and be ready to set the hook.

In many of my intense formative fishing years my data showed that my trophy bass were 3 or 4 percent of my total. After many seasons and following the tried and true baits, tactics, and techniques in this book currently and for the last several years my ratio of trophy bass (over five pounds) is TEN PERCENT of my total catch. I'm catching smaller numbers but consistently BIG bass.

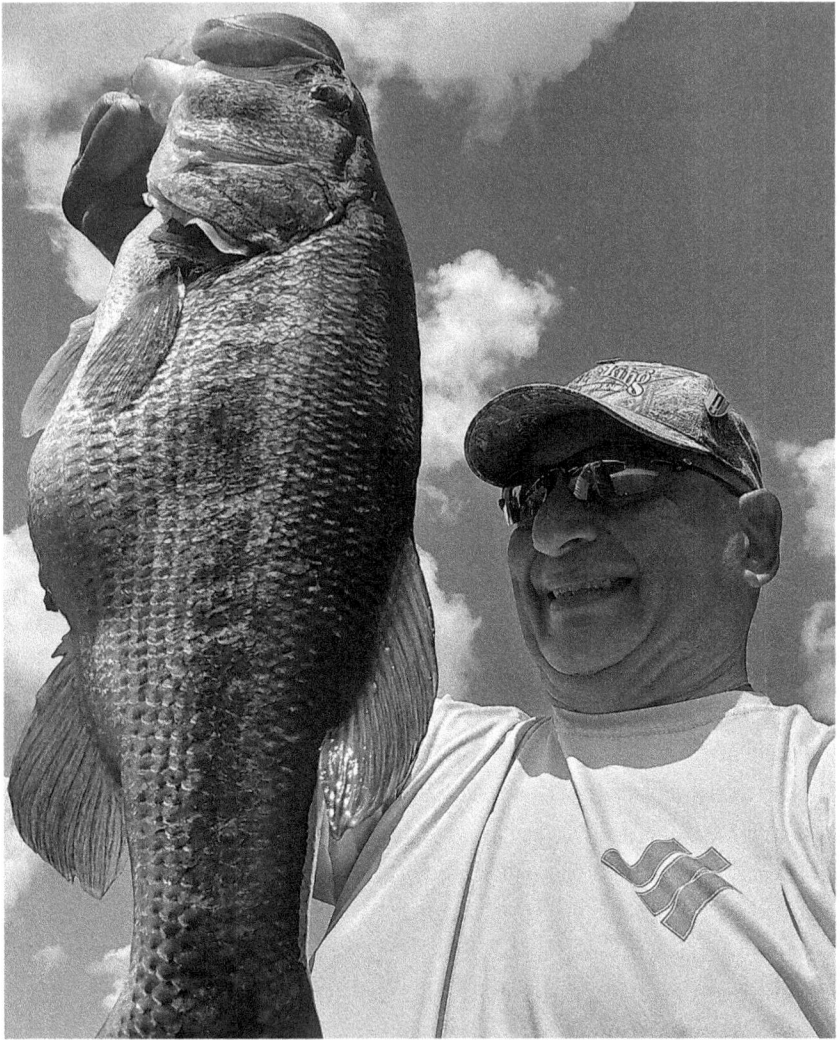

5

Baiting Up

Early in my fishing career I wandered the aisles of every store that had fishing tackle. Department stores, big and small sporting goods places, isolated country establishments, even out of the way gas stations might have that *magic lure* unavailable somewhere else. *Oh, that looks good I'll grab a couple of those. This looks like the bait I saw on television; didn't I see this in that magazine, all reasons to add a lure(s) to a growing stockpile of bass baits.*

I believed at the time the person with the most tackle was going to be the bass expert. I walked into the garage of a fishing mentor I had met, and there was a pegboard full of bass fishing baits. Another corner of the room housed dozens of rod and reel combos! I thought silently, *I know this guy is a doctor; I can't financially keep up with him.*

After many years and several dollars, I came to the conclusion that even though I had all these lures in several tackle boxes; some looked so good I couldn't bear to tie them on. Others rested in the trays of an enormous green monstrous multi-tray, pull-out, expanding box that gave me the false sense of being prepared for any situation. After many seasons I decided that actually the less I carried the more confidence in the lures I had, and realistically I already knew what I was going to use. I had baits that I caught a few fish on almost every time. This small selection of lures could be carried comfortably in a box that resembled the old-style metal

21

hinged-lid lunch boxes carried by the common working man. Thus came the *one-year rule*, a self-imposed guideline which made me a better bass angler. Here it is—I could have as much tackle as I wanted, but if I didn't tie it on, it never got wet, or if I didn't catch a fish on it, then it had to come out. After about three years I had a couple of one-sided plastic tackle boxes that had me ready for almost any situation. I carry a small assortment of soft plastics to use as bait trailers on jig or spinners and to be rigged as Texas rigs, shakey heads, or on a standard leadhead, and that's pretty much it. I do change out colors, add or subtract seasonal baits, or make adjustment based off new water and various weather conditions.

A specific example would be crankbaits. I'm fond of the 1.5 square bill from Strike King. I've enjoyed great success in the magic depths of 3–8 feet with this lure. I always carry three colors: #584 Oyster—a perfect shad matching color; a #563 orange belly craw to mimic crawdads; and the highly visible chartreuse/black back #535. Those have earned their way into my every-trip tackle boxes.

The question you should ask yourself in choosing an artificial bait is, what does it mimic? Does it move like the real thing? A study of a shallow water creek brought this lesson. Minnows (there are several varieties) essentially move three ways, they swim along casually, they dart erratically when being pursued, and exhibit a dying flutter when injured. The darting motion is what sends fish into a chase/catch (cat and mouse scenario) mode, the fluttering/dying look brings out the apex predatory instinct of a bass. Make your bait look like this, and eventually you'll get bit.

Another specific example is the crawfish. A highly prized food source by all the bass species, the crawfish exhibits distinctive locomotion. On the bottom a crawfish crawls along moving FOR-WARD. When threatened, in an effort to escape, they move in two or three quick bursts propelling themselves BACKWARD. When they come to rest, they raise their claws in a defensive posture. If you ever see a crawfish with one claw or two different sizes, they have lost one (likely to a fish) and can slowly regenerate a new

one. There are many more examples, including shad, frogs, snakes, and others.

Bait Size

Some folks stand by the concept that large baits catch large fish. *Always* and *never* are strong words, but one can make the case for size matters. Keep in mind every year some crappie angler catches a monster bass on tiny baits designed to fool a panfish. On the other hand, it's become fashionable for California, Florida, and Texas bass-chasers to use giant, hand-poured, soft swim baits while targeting huge bass. For the average bass fishermen, standard size lures are tied on to the end of their line. The biggest bass eventually experience a phenomenon which might lend credence to the large bait theory. Little bass zip through schools of minnows, shad, and other forage and get most everything that is vacuumed into their mouths. As bass get bigger, the expanse between their gill and body get larger. The same bass now swallows a mouth full of minnows but some escape because the gill rakers (the red spiny appendages) are further apart, thus little food sources can get away, BUT the bigger ones are devoured without any problems. The bass is conditioned to pursue bigger food sources.

There's also the trait common to many of the superior of the species in which the payoff is bigger when they go after the larger meal. The same amount of energy is expended, but the nutritional value is increased. In a scientific attempt to understand the bass, it's important at times to lean on the data. Studies have shown that bass can consume 12 percent of their body weight and digest it in 6–12 hours. It's also important to note that water temperature will dictate the speed of complete digestion. Who of us hasn't landed a fish with a shad or crawfish in its gullet? There's also the fish that are spitting up several shad at being stressed as they're played in or the evidence in a live well showing stomach contents being the recent meal regurgitated by the fish. Remember, bass are opportunistic feeders, eating what's readily available, close by

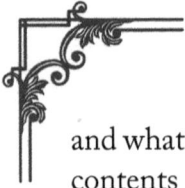

and what they can fit in their stomach cavities. Studies on stomach contents routinely show a high percentage of shad, often 57% or more (because shad are the most available forage) and roughly 33% crawfish depending again on the availability. In the world of the bass everything is on the menu.

Color Controversy

A recent peak at a top lure companies catalog revealed an astounding number of colors to choose from including 62 soft plastic colors and 70 different hard plastic colors.

THEORY: Different colors have a higher appeal to bass and other fish mainly because of various water colors and other factors. A few variables might include the amount of *stain* produced by rain and the level of light penetration based on cloud cover or wind.

Because bass feed primarily by sight this can be vital to fooling a few fish. Bass have a 300% range of peripheral vision and because of this there are times I try to present a limited look at certain baits to draw a reaction type strike. For example, if my target is heavy cover and I'm using a buzzbait, I throw well past the cover and try to bring the bait past the fish where I believe it offers a short back to forward look at the lure. The lure comes past the fish from the rear and requires a quick decision as to whether to hit or pass. The physical composition of the bass' eyes show that they pick up the colors red and green well with difficulty in differentiating the darker shades.

Note: Most anglers should fish focused on waters from one to fifteen feet. With the exception of smallmouth, I've never caught a big bass in more then 12 feet of water. One more consideration is the depth that you are presenting your artificial lure. In depths of more than 15 feet, colors begin to change for the bass. Red changes to a brownish tint, then yellow, orange, green, and purple

and then even in clear water at 30 feet most colors turn to shades of gray to black.

TROPHY TIP: In murky to muddy water, a red crankbait is more visible to bass and can be deadly for shallow water fish around heavy cover. Replacing a spinnerbait blade with a red one is also an option. One of my favorite spinnerbait hacks is to replace the back blade with a copper-colored oversized willowleaf blade. This particular alteration has helped me fool three largemouth over nine pounds. No red blades? An inexpensive can of spray paint solves that problem.

6

Digging Way Down into Details

If you like to try live bait fish for bass, here's my take on selections. Get the biggest live bait you can buy/catch. The biggest bait tempts the larger fish because it looks live, moves like live, shows fear like live, tastes like live, and all these add up to potentially taking a trophy. I've done very well with big creek minnows, live bluegill, crawfish, and others. The use of "wild caught" minnows, shiners, or shad possesses one distinct advantage, the natural predator/prey relationship. I've used the big minnows fished under a natural cork float and many times watched as the bait got *nervous* indicated by the float bobbing and moving off swiftly into escape mode, the float would take off with the bass in hot pursuit. Often the bait would jump completely out of the water trying to escape the hard charging bass. Story note: It doesn't end well for the bait.

Two major factors in presenting artificial baits are the categories they all have; the attraction factors, and the strike triggering factors. Bright colors, larger sizes, noise making capabilities, and a predictable action are the factors of attraction. These are the components to getting the attention of the fish, but just getting their attention is of little value if you can't seal the deal—get them to hit. What makes a bass bite? The triggers are natural swimming motions, more neutral colors, natural shapes, realistic profiles, shapes that are easily swallowed, and random action.

It's worth noting both these attributes are directed toward visual

appeal of the members of the bass family. These considerations, in my opinion, are the most important in choosing and using any artificial bait in the pursuit of giant bass.

Making Sense Of Senses

Giving extreme credence to the importance of the eyesight of bass, we can move to the lateral line which helps detect vibration and aids in the feeding ability of the fish also in the possibility of sensing underwater predators. As far as hearing, bass have internal ears and do hear reasonably well, and this, coupled with their other sensory abilities, gives them a good set of survival instincts.

Now on to a pair of my favorite fallacies, some based on science and others off a common sense approach to landing lunkers, the sense of taste, and the sense of smell in the bass family. Something I had previously published spoke to the factor of taste in fishing in general. Yes, bass do have the ability to taste, but it's NOT why they strike an artificial bait. Taste occurs AFTER the hit. Does taste matter? Only from the perspective that they might hold on to a bait longer if they identify a pleasing flavor. For people convinced that that taste is vital, I have one question: Where is the bait when the bass tastes it? It's already in its mouth. SET THE HOOK!

For old timers, there were pork frogs that came in jars and also bottled in salt brine. Even now many soft plastic baits are laden with salt. In freshwater and salt water fish and their food, there is as much as 1% salt in their blood composition, therefore salt is a familiar taste for gamefish. As for the sense of smell in bass, documented tests reveal there's very little ability to smell in the bass family. Their smell is limited naturally by the lack of *folds* believed to be 10 percent less that other wild creatures with diminished possession of what is necessary to be an efficient sniffer.

If you are fan of the scented baits, one thing you can do to maximize this aspect of soft plastic lures is prior to attaching your *smelly* bait, place it in between the palms of your hands and rub them together vigorously—the heat generated will bring out the

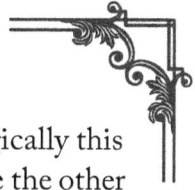

highest level of smell. Also, it should be pointed out logically this only becomes useful in very muddy water where I believe the other senses are heightened.

THEORY: It's a matter of chronological use of the available sensory traits. Using whitetail deer as another example of chorological senses, if a deer smells your presence, even from a distance you'll likely never see it. Much like your family dog, as puppies their whole world is their nose. If you pass the smell test with deer next up is hearing, then on to visual scanning of an area that they are familiar with from being in their range or territory.

Dismissing the importance of the bass's dependence on visual clues is a critical error in the search for the biggest bass. The other senses pale in comparison and come into play under the most adverse of conditions. Keep in mind while you're in recreational mode, the bass is in survival mode.

All baits, even those that might be considered in the same category, require a closer look. How about crankbaits? One distinction I made years ago is the difference between the baits constructed of plastic or wood. For years there were cedar and balsa *plugs* and then years later the advent of hard, brittle plastic, and eventually the modern-day floater/diver plastic cranking baits—there is a difference in the way they perform. The plastic lures are molded with an air chamber. The ways the baits run are dictated by length of cast, line diameter, AND, in my opinion, water temperature. The colder water achieves one range of depth while warm water another. The hollow body chamber has air inside and hot air rises. My suspicion is the plastic crankbait runs deeper in cold water and inherently shallower in hot water. Wood most likely runs more consistent, BUT both catch their share of bass. The wood body may be more durable, but the plastic lips on either are vulnerable to rocks, docks, and being smashed on the surface by frustrated anglers trying to remove hooked moss, weeds, or foreign objects.

The profile of any bait is also worth consideration. There's the long, thin body of a minnow imitator or the fat wide look of a lipless crankbait. Eye appeal in different situations can make a difference. Fish feeding on shad, bluegill, or even the reluctantly fed upon crappie would recognize the profile of a bait (live or artificial) as a potential good size meal. Crappie, because of their large spiny fins, are not a target food for fish. Often bass are found floating choked with a crappie lodged in its throat.

Coupled with profile is the action of the bait. The predictable, mechanical action of a bait can make it challenging in the waters that receive a high degree of fishing pressure with the fish often getting the same visual. It's one of the reasons anglers catch giant bass at night. The clues are not as recognizable to fish as they would be in clear water and bright sunny conditions. Spinnerbaits and crankbaits come to mind immediately in this discussion.

To combat this, I often modify these baits. Simple changes have produced great results. For example, on my spinners, I commonly throw willowleaf spinnerbaits. I have willow/Colorado combination, double willow, and some older baits marketed under the name "quad shad" equipped with four blades (the original A-rig concept). The willowleaf blade provides the maximum amount of flash and the least amount of vibration.

A common error in the discussion on spinnerbaits is that the blade vibrates. Sorry, NO. The arm of the bait vibrates solely dependent on the shape and size of the blade. The blade displaces water.

I normally modify my spinnerbait to just the back blade, clipping the clevis that holds the front blade closest to the leadhead, offering a different look and another visual presentation which can be new to the bass. With my crankbaits, a regular non-fishing day activity is changing out the front treble hook to the same size as a blood red model. The red treble is subtle but gives the fish an intentionally limited hint of red, a predatory triggering color. The gills of a bluegill trying to escape are bright red from the effort exerted in the escape attempt. The effectiveness in this modification comes

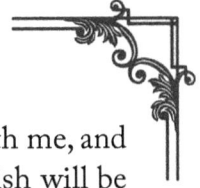

with my standard offer to the nonbelievers that fish with me, and I'll wager a one dollar bet on the hook the crankbait fish will be caught on—it's normally about 80 to 90 percent of the time on the front red hook.

THEORY: I want the fish to hit the front hook because most logically it's going to be a better connection with the fighting bass. Again, appealing to the visual sense.

TROPY TIP: Knowing the forage base in the waters you fish is important. Most bigger waters have shad, minnows, and crawfish. Matching the color of the bait is great, but matching the motion AND upsizing the offering positions you to fool a trophy fish. Bass opt for the bigger meal if they have to expend the same amount of energy to catch the food. This is why flipping and pitching into heavy cover works, the fish is presented with what appears to be an easy food source that is readily available, it's a meal delivered to them that they don't have to chase down.

7

Developing a Feel for Fish

Because of their importance, these next three component segments will come up often: The three "Rs"—Retrieve Speed, Random Action, and Resistance. These factors to me, are vital to finding, fooling, and landing BIG bass. My lack of electronic assistance has created in me an approach that relies on gut feel, experience, sensory observation (mostly visual clues), and natural instinct. Clear water allows for some great lessons.

Retrieve Speed—While it's believed that bass can swim in bursts of 12–15 miles an hour, they like other wild things, inherently understand that a short chase in the pursuit of food sources pays off rather than a long protracted pursuit that doesn't supply the same or more energy than expended. In the work world it's described as ROI or return on investment. This is also why a bass will snub a smaller bait and choose a larger version of the same forage. So a key to the catch is making your bait look real but also making it look as something easily caught—slow, wounded, or just venturing too close to the apex predator, a big bass. This is why retrieve speed is so important. Too fast, in most instances, looks like a hard target to catch up with and is allowed to leave. Some of the factors in determining retrieve speed are 1. Water temperature 2. Water color 3. Other external condition like moon phase or wind, cloud cover etc. Water temperature sets the stage for digestive speed—the quicker the fish digests, the sooner they will feed again. Pre-spawn and fall feeding are examples of when bass will gorge themselves on anything they can track down. Water color determines the ability of the fish to see potential food sources.

THEORY: dirty water fish will generally move shallow especially in current found in river systems. They will often stage down stream from fixed objects such as manmade things: bridge pilings, boat docks, and wing dams, or natural objects like submerged trees and boulder rock. A side note, bends in moving water should be recognized and adjustments made. Largemouth will often choose inside bends because of less current, while smallmouth like cooler (moving) water and may likely set up on outside bends with a little more current. Smallmouth will stage behind midstream objects and "pick off" food that wanders into their strike zone (more on strike zone later).

Random Action—This is at the core of my belief in tactics that consistently fool big bass. Based on my experiences and those of others, I can say that random action is at the top of the list of qualities I look at in choosing and using artificial lures. I directly attribute random action to being the reason bass, especially BIG ones, don't "catch on" to that category of baits and will hit them often and repeatedly. A poll of some of the best anglers in the world (some famous; others local or regional experts) shows an undeniable similar result in using a certain type of lure to catch their biggest bass. Here's a list of a few of the fishing folks I reached out to in order to test my beliefs.

- Denny Brauer, legendary tournament fisherman, expert jig fisherman—his biggest bass was a 15 ½ pound largemouth from Lake Amistad in Texas, taken on a Denny Brauer structure jig, Rage chunk both in color green pumpkin.
- Doug Hannon, BIG bass expert with more than 500 bass over 10 pounds to his credit, inventor-author, his huge bass was 17 lbs. on 10-inch worm from the Florida Everglades.

- Charlie Evans, long-time tournament pro, he landed a 12 pound 15 ounce bass on a black/blue jig trailed by a BIG Zoom chunk (green pumpkin, AGAIN)
- Lou Williams, long-time legendary bass expert calling Pickwick Lake his home waters, he has a 10 pound 5 ounce largemouth to his credit caught on a 5-inch white curly tail grub, and an enormous, Tennessee trophy 8 pound 5 ounce smallmouth landed on a jerkbait.
- Dear friend, author, and avid angler Michael Vines loves and lives for the frog bite, his biggest bass came on a soft plastic frog and weighed eight pounds.
- Karl Kalonka, Canadian angler, TV host, and fishing industry expert fooled a 9 pound largemouth on a Strike King Jig/KVD chunk. His best smallmouth was a 7 pounder on a spinnerbait.
- My own best BIG bass catch was an 11 pound 3 ounce river largemouth caught on ⅜th oz. Strike King jig color #8 Texas craw, Rage tail craw in color #229 roadkill, and an 8 pound Canadian smallmouth on a spinnerbait.
- Steve Parks, the man who developed the Ragetail line of soft plastic and who has dozens of double digit bass to his credit, landed a monstrous 15 pound 7 ounce largemouth on a ten-inch Ragetail Anaconda Worm.
- And then there is the Legendary Bill Dance, who recalled a 14 pound one ounce largemouth that inhaled a free falling Bass Pro Shops double-bladed spinnerbait, and an eight pound three ounce huge smallmouth that hit a Little George tail spinner. He was quick to point out another eight plus pound smallmouth that came from my backyard Woods Reservoir—eight pounds one ounce while night fishing and again on a spinnerbait.

Two things jump out at me when going through this list or discussing with people the background story to their biggest bass, most of the fish were caught on what I categorize as "feel" baits.

Feel baits are baits that are moved with the rod, possess random action, and are silent. Each of these qualities plays into my belief of a specific system that positions you to catch a true trophy. I am in no way saying this is the *only* way to a big fish, but there is evidence that these types of traits are desirable in the search for a giant.

Years ago, I had access to a great fishin' hole. It regularly produced big bass, and I had previously used a fish tagging system. You had a small spaghetti-like, pliable 3-inch rubber tube with a consecutive number, my name and phone number. The tag had a small barb on one end which allowed you to insert the barb behind the dorsal fin of the bass and give that specific fish an identity. If caught by someone they could contact me, and I could get data about the length, weight, and any other details. I tagged one fish that weighed about four pounds, and I fished this body of water regularly with a wide variety of baits. I caught that particular tagged fish four more times over the next two years and despite the fact that I had thrown everything in the tackle box *and* each time I caught that fish it was on a jig or plastic worm! Coincidence? I doubt it.

Resistance—Defined as *fought, opposed, withstood* in the dictionary. My definition, for our purposes, is the sensation you feel when your bait stops, the swimming motion stops, or you feel some degree of tension at the other end of your line. For the feel baits, this is critical. I'd venture to say most people would communicate that they wondered what a "pick up" felt like when they first started fishing. Even after years many anglers would relay the story about "I just felt something different, it felt like somebody had cut my bait off, I saw my line swimming off." Each of these is accurate. If you're waiting for a pronounced thump or a hard tug, you're going to miss a bunch of fish. The charm of fishing what I refer to as feel baits is that instantaneous high of knowing a bass just inhaled your lure and preparing to set the hook. Even though I do it regularly, I don't advise "checking" the fish—lifting the rod tip until you feel steady pressure. You'll lose a lot of fish because of your indecision, and the fish realizing something isn't right will quickly reject the

bait. Take out the mental highlighter, commit this to memory… if you feel anything different, anything at all, SET THE HOOK! Set it hard and often, it's free! Work to develop a sensitivity in your hands that will transmit to your brain the signal, fish on. More on the family of feel baits later.

TROPHY TIP: In choosing a hook for Texas rigging a soft plastic bait, make sure the hook is sized correctly for the thickness of the bait. While a 3/0 hook may be ideal for a straight tail worm, you would miss most of those same fish when presenting a flipping tube or a frog. I'd recommend a 6/0 hook for these bigger baits. Carry several sizes and make sure when "skin hooking" the lure that the point will pop through easily and thereby penetrate the jaw of your fish.

8

Chasing The Records

The dream of many is to catch and cash in on a world record bass. Surely fame and fortune in cash, promotions, and endorsements awaits the record holders. Let's take a look at that aspect of bass angling, one which is not without controversy. The International Game Fish Association (IGFA) is the governing body that makes the final determination in the establishment of world record fish.

The Spotted AKA Kentucky record was set in Northern California where a bass weighing 11 lb 4 oz was caught. It was 24 ¼ inches long with a girth of 20 ¾ inches. It is the current mark and qualified under the most stringent requirements of the IGFA. Nick Dulleck chased after the record for quite a while and was using a Dirty Jigs football jig with a Yamamoto Twin Tail trailer, Feb. 12th, 2015 on New Bullards Bar Reservoir in Northern California. The Spotted AKA Kentucky bass has a small group of ardent followers but doesn't draw the attention of the other two major species the largemouth and smallmouth. While this is a monumental catch, much more attention is focused on the world record largemouth.

The most revered record is the Largemouth bass that was caught in a backwater off Montgomery Lake in Georgia in June of 1932. This fish eclipsed the Florida bass caught by Fritz Friebel in 1923 and weighed 20 lb 2 oz. In May of 1923, Friebel went fishing with a couple of friends in Big Fish Lake, and he landed the 20-pound,

2-ounce largemouth bass that measured 31 inches long with a 27-inch girth. Almost nine years later George Perry would set the new standard, and that world record bass, weighing 22 pounds and 4 ounces, has stood the test of time—over 80 years.

Controversy over bait has arisen. I interviewed owner Carl H. (Harry) Heinzerling, who stated the bait that fooled the record fish came from the Creek Chub Company of Garret Indiana, and it was a Wiggle fish in #2401 Perch pattern—recent suggestions claim that the bait which was described as a topwater Creek Chub Fintail Shiner is the lure used that day to make the catch. One look at the lip on this bait shown in a photo reveals it certainly IS NOT a top water lure furthering the erroneous claim of a different lure.

Georgia Historical Society stated the bass was 32 ½ inches in length and 28 ½ inches in girth and was caught on Perry's only lure, a Creek Chub lure a "Fintail Shiner in Silver Shiner." Years ago in my phone conversations with one of the original owners, Harry Heinzerling, he again stated repeatedly that the bait was a Creek Chub Wiggle Fish in color pattern 2401 Natural Perch. I confirmed this in several subsequent interviews with Heinzerling.

Japanese angler Manabu Kurita has tied Mr. Perry's world record largemouth bass, his bass from Lake Biwa in Japan weighed 22 pounds, 5 ounces, the bass was bigger than George Perry's bass, *but* IGFA regulations stipulate that the new record must surpass the current record by more than two ounces. Official Kurita's record fish is considered a tie. For years several states, in my opinion, have tried to "raise" a world record bass. Most notably California has done a few things to try to *manufacture* a world record largemouth. Stocking highly nutritious rainbow trout provides a high-powered food source for the California bass population. There are also restrictions on some of the most likely trophy waters limiting the available days and number of anglers allowed on the potential record-breaking waters.

Smallmouth—A freak 11-pound, 15-ounce smallmouth bass was hauled in by David L Hayes. Hayes. He caught his behemoth

smallmouth bass out of Dale Hollow Lake that borders Kentucky and Tennessee in 1955. To be more precise on July 9, 1955, at around 10 a.m., Hayes made his historical catch while trolling a plug, specifically a #600 series pearl Bomber on 20-pound test line. The massive smallmouth measured 27 inches in length and with a 21 ⅔-inch girth. With the hype about the possible bass records, this is one I believe will never be broken! Water quality, fishing pressure, natural mortality, mishandling of landed fish, and people keeping fish to mount or consume all play a part, in my opinion, in this record being around forever. A Mr. John Gorman caught a 10-pound, 14-ounce smallmouth in April of 1969. Pickwick Lake (Tennessee) and Dale Hollow (Tennessee and Kentucky) both have produced true trophies, but nothing has come close to the Hayes bass, one-ounce shy of twelve pounds. Only six other smallmouth bass have had their weight certified as being over ten pounds, two by the most famous smallmouth expert ever, Bill Westmoreland. Another interesting fact is that 13 of the top 25 smallmouth bass landed and weight certified came from Tennessee waters.

One key factor seldom mentioned is that both major species, largemouth and smallmouth, bass world records were caught during the summer months!

Let's look at the barriers to breaking the records.

Water quality contaminations—Mercury levels, pesticides, and other chemicals are problematic in some bodies of water. Nature and natural elements allow healing and cleansing but there remain dramatic and residual effects on fish and wildlife.

Fishing pressure—Fish become "conditioned" and will avoid certain baits, sights, and sounds. It's a survival trait. It's likely many fish (and other forms of wildlife) die eventually after being exposed to external influences, and they feed, breed, travel avoiding contact with humans.

Natural mortality and aging populations are often attributed to people but not wild things; but in the world, everything has a "life expectancy." It may be considered sad, but it's the way of the

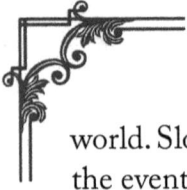

world. Slowdowns, disease, and other facets of life and death mean the eventual demise of living things.

Mishandling of landed fish is a problem especially in the summer. Mishandling would include deep hooking of a bass, removing the slime coat which causes a bacterial infection much like a burn to a human. Touching the eyes or the gills is a danger also. In the summer, with dissolved oxygen at a yearly low, fish can be stressed by being caught or placed for a prolonged period of time in a live well. This often leads to delayed mortality where even though a bass may swim off, it will die in the next 24 to 48 hours.

People keeping trophy fish to mount is a problem that has decreased because of the cost and the availability of realistic replicas. In years past many anglers would hang every big bass caught on the wall of their trophy room, but we've become more aware of the need for release of the true trophy fish. I recall from a photo published year ago a Florida fisherman who proclaimed he had a goal of catching a world record bass. In his den were several mounted fish, every bass he had landed over ten pounds, many on the 12 to 15-pound category. I thought, *you might have the potential world record on your wall.* In all fairness, any fish you catch legally or ethically is yours to do as you choose, but you want to consider the long-term result of your decision either way.

Hook em' and cook em'—People want fish to eat. The consumption of the catch isn't often considered a threat, but over-harvest or the removal of the bigger fish changes the fishery. Removing the genetically superior fish reduces the gene pool to the ordinary population. I was informed about the highest sales years for the Creek Chub Bait Company in a long-ago discussion with one of the former owners, Harry Heinzerling. He explained that, in the early 1940s, they produced and sold more baits than at any other time. This confused me because of the link to the time period in our history known as the Great Depression. What made dramatic sense to me was he explained that people were fishing for food not for fun!

It's worth noting that all the same factors, the afore mentioned barriers would, in my opinion, affect the population of trophy bass in any waters.

TROPHY TIP: The biggest bass are the superior of the species and the apex predator. Successfully releasing those fish is important to the health of that body of water and increases the chances that more true trophy bass will continue to be available.

9

Patterns

My favorite description of a pattern goes like this; the first fish is luck, the second fish is a clue, and the third fish a pattern.

One of the joys of fishing is recognizing a pattern and using this new found knowledge in catching great numbers of fish by applying the specific aspects of the pattern. Steep banks, submerged wood, aquatic vegetation, boat docks, points, chunk rock, or even combinations of objects or conditions that are holding bass all constitute a pattern. Often, through the course of a day, patterns can change, and this requires adjustments from the angler. Some patterns are repeatable on certain bodies of water and through certain seasons. This is why I have for years kept a journal of my trips.

A large dose of logic comes in handy also. A question was posed to me during a fishing seminar at an outdoor show; "If I pull into a cover and there's a hundred trees in the area, which should I fish first?" After a moment I replied, "I would find a cove with ten trees and fish it. The cove with a hundred tree probably has fifteen fish in it. The area with ten trees probably has eight fish in it. In my opinion the smaller area would be easier to fish effectively. If you were committed to the cove with a hundred, I'd fish the edges first as a more likely way to develop a solid pattern. I'd also consider the presence of bait and the access to deep water."

A fond fishing memory came with the accidental discovery of a late fall pattern. A three-day warming weather trend hit, and

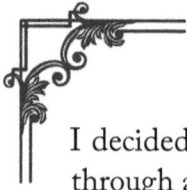

I decided to try my luck. While fishing a small lake, I had gone through a progression of bass baits with no luck. I determined to try one more lure before calling it a day. I tied on a #300 C, silver black back A.C. Shiner (a minnow plug) and began random casts paralleling the shoreline. No hits. Out of desperation I heaved my bait toward the middle of the little lake, and after a couple of top water twitches started winding back my bait and inadvertently paused for a moment. When I started my retrieve, a solid three-pound bass hit! Another cast imitating the previous retrieve and another fish; this one about four pounds. The next 30 minutes are what dreams are made of. I landed eight more bass using the cast, quick start, pause and repeat with several between five and seven pounds! My quest to develop patterns was born that day.

This, among other factors, is one of the critical steps to "cracking the code" for BIG bass. To consistently hook and land the biggest bass you must be aware of all the details to build a foundation for trophy bass fishing. If someone goes long enough and often, they'll catch a few good fish even if by accident, but to build the confidence and trust your intuitive skills is vital to catching bigger bass in any season, on any waters, and using just a few techniques.

There are many more interesting and relatable patterns which would apply to several bodies of water. Some of the most notable are big fallen trees that are resting at roughly a 90-degree angle on a steep bank. This happened in many instances on rivers and areas where there was a narrowing of the waters. I have seen this situation produce an unbelievable square bill crankbait pattern. A long cast parallel to the bank, casting upstream or above the current flow and well past the fallen tree with a medium retrieve and bumping the wood produces a predictable deflection bite. When you find this, it can be a banner bass day.

Another huge pattern would be edges. Because bass, like many other fish and even wildlife, relate heavily to edges, they deserve attention. Look for opportunities to work edges because truly big bass use them as a repeating lifestyle whether to feed, migrate, or

stage. Edges can be characterized as existing as shorelines, the trunk of a downed tree, the bottom, a dock or even the surface. Bass use them to pin prey to an inescapable scenario, they've got no place to go. I would bet that everyone has had an instance where reeling back they reach the edge of the shoreline (for bank anglers) or even the side of your boat and have a fish lunge at your bait. The perceived prey has nowhere to go. Bass pushing bait to the surface use this tactic to attack schools of shad or other forage—the surface is the ultimate edge because of gravity. What goes up eventually must come down.

Current, especially for smallmouth and river resident fish, is a strong pattern everywhere there is moving water. Regardless of size, the current pattern holds true from a small creek to a major river. At times the stronger the current the more likely the pattern. Fish normally (notice I didn't say always) face into current. Because of the way they're built physically it makes it easier and they're fighting the current flow less. Often the fish will stage behind any object that lessens the current or redirects the flow and delivers food. Smallmouth are notorious for this, and midstream riffles or any object becomes a feeding zone or a resting spot. In heavy river current, I search out backwaters where fish can rest and ambush unsuspecting food sources seeking a break from the fast waters. A more remote spot with less current and heavy cover can yield a giant bass.

During the spring or any cooler weather and water conditions, it's advisable to consider the Northwest side of the lake. Because the sun rises in the East and sets in the West, the Northwest side should get the most sunlight. A few degrees difference in the surface water temperature will draw bait and bass. As an added attraction, if there is gravel, chunk rock, an old road bed, or even a concrete launch ramp this could be the ticket to cold water bass. The presence of two or more desirable elements would be describes as a pattern within a pattern, these are a little trickier to recognize but are golden opportunities in difficult conditions but may be

harder to replicate. A favorite of mine and very common is the presence of weedy vegetation and wood in the form of stumps, submerged trees, or man-made stake beds. Two very desirable elements could be a solid set up for a BIG bass.

From a seasonal perspective, aquatic vegetation throughout the spring and summer can be challenging but highly productive. Weed choked areas may require a slow methodical presentation in small openings and edges. Lily pads for the frog fishing folks are fun but can be frustrating. Vegetation of almost any variety offers three of the basic bass needs: oxygen, cover, and food. Don't pass up the chance to work the weeds. I fish weeds through the year. Green is good'; brown is bad.

Other potential patterns include, but are not limited to, inflowing creeks, points, creek channels, weed natural corners, and specific depths. Even the presence of birds such as sea gulls, herons, and more signal the gathering of schools of minnows or shad, another great natural clue. It's important to keep in mind several patterns are likely emerging all over the same body of water. Variables like surface temperature, various water color, available forage, unique depth, cover, or vegetation could all contribute to reliable patterns present on the same or nearby waters.

Rick Clunn recently revealed a seasonal strategy that helped him win his first Bassmaster Classic. In the first three Bassmaster classics he had found out the winning stringer all came from competitors going to the backs of creeks in the lakes. Then each year the classics were held in October, and that year was no exception. In 1976 Clunn landed one ounce shy of 60 pounds of largemouth bass from the three day event on Lake Guntersville in Alabama fishing the backs of creeks with, what else, a spinnerbait.

Don't discount some crazy unconventional patterns. While fishing from a boat in a small, clear, back water cove I watched as carp (yep, carp) were flipping over rocks to catch the crawfish hiding under the flat rocks. Unbelievably I watched as bass moved in and began waiting for the carp to turn over the rocks and then

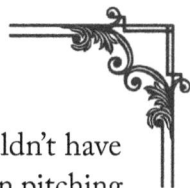

systematically zoom in to snatch the crawfish. If I wouldn't have seen it, I would never had believed it. Oh yeah, I also began pitching crawfish colored jigs into the area and caught several bass!

Another accidental, but often repeated, pattern is that of game fish raiding the spawning beds of other species. I've caught multiple smallmouth bass in early summer in a place that shocked me. Fishing bluegill beds in eight feet of water, and *bang*, a smallmouth nailed a small tube bait. Another and another followed by a 12-pound channel catfish all raiding bluegill beds and hitting small tubes that matched the bluegill fry. In another instance I caught two giant crappies (each over 16 inches) doing exactly the same thing, moving into shallow water beds to eat baby bluegill! On another occasion I was watching a bass waiting on the perimeter of a big bedding area, it was sizing up the menu of little and adult bluegill occupying the area. I cast past the beds and brought a buzzbait directly through and saw bluegill scattering and a giant bass exploded on this intruder!

One of my most memorable pattern discoveries came during a fishing tournament. My go-to presentation had been the pitching technique I had used for several seasons. Fishing out of town, on a strange lake, and as a co-angler we started conventionally and did nothing for a few hours. After a bit of convincing, we made a move to shallower water on the lake which had been receiving a fair amount of pressure. The rest was history. I started loading the live well. With a heavy bag of fish and standing on the stage I was being interviewed by the weigh-in master of ceremonies. At the interview he pointed out that I had had a pretty big day, was cashing a nice check, and he wanted to know the secret.

"So, do you mind telling us how you caught your fish?" was the question.

My reply, "I was pitching a black and blue jig."

He remarked further, "Well I think a lot of people were throwing black and blue jigs, anything else?"

I responded, "I was throwing to boat docks."

Again he countered with, "Several people were casting to docks."

Slyly I admitted, "I was throwing under boat docks with spider webs."

He looked at me and questioned, "Spider Webs?"

Laughing, I replied, "Yeah, no one had thrown under there in several days!"

Patterns!

TROPHY TIP: On windy days, go to the bank receiving the wind and break out the spinnerbaits. The churning of the waters starts the feeding cycle by moving tiny food sources throughout the waters and bringing in feeding baitfish, craws, and other bass foods. The bass move in to take advantage of the shallow water buffet, a variety of spinners will work, and feeding binges along the bank are often the reward for fishing the wind.

10

Best Days

The best days are the stories legends are made of, providing lasting memories and day dreams. My best days are the ones when I've wished the sun wouldn't set. Surprisingly enough some of my best days weren't under perfect conditions—wind, rain, equipment failures, or even hours of no activity somehow turned into fishing/catching memories.

For years I fished almost anytime when time was available. I planned short trips to close to home waters or to smaller lakes and ponds with the idea I'd be able to cover water in time to get home in a reasonable manner for family activities or work requirements. Early on my fishing, like most people, was limited to weekends, and even then with a hectic work schedule if I wanted to fish, I had to fish late at night.

I often hear anglers discuss their plans to fish when the conditions are what they would deem as perfect. This is what some people think of as the criteria for the *perfect day*—air temperature around 75, surface water temperatures 65–70 degrees, a slight wind, clear water, and a full moon. Good luck. You'll probably get these four or five times a year.

It was late November 1978. I was living in Missouri and I had launched my boat and was moving up the north bank of 85-acre Lake Wauwanoka. The fall season, a full moon, and the possibility of a fish were calling me. I had access to this lake only because I had plunked down $500 for a second tier ½ acre lot with hopes of building a retirement home there. Propelled by only a small trolling motor and braving less than perfect conditions, I found myself bucking a cold wind and even colder air temperatures. Knowing my fishing season would quickly be over because the little lake would soon be iced over sent me on a mission to catch a few more fish.

I was casting one of these new-fangled jigs and after hearing and reading about the setup, had settled on the pro's recommendation: a black ½ ounce jig with a #1 Big Daddy Uncle Josh pork frog trailer. The sun had already set, but I was determined to continue even though my battery power was dwindling. There was a particular rock drop-off where the water went from three feet quickly to about eight feet, and it seemed a likely largemouth hangout.

Casts one, two, and three went unrewarded, and truly I wasn't even sure I would know what a bite felt like on this unproven bait. Then, just at dusk, my retrieve was interrupted by a slow persistent tug. Rearing back, the short stout rod bent under the weight of something I hoped to be a bass. My drag on the Garcia 5500C reel was set way too tight but had been untested by the cookie cutter 12-inch bass I was used to catching. The rod, line, and I were all straining to winch this creature to the surface. Eventually the biggest bass I had ever personally seen rolled on the surface, I immediately I grabbed my net, which was a poor man's version of a landing net—a tiny trout net attached with electrical tape to a bamboo pole—and slid it under my prize. Protruding from the mouth and down in the throat of my fish was the tail of another fish which proved to be a 10-inch channel catfish.

After removing the partially digested catfish, I found myself struggling for breath. Still stunned by my catch, I trolled to the first house I saw with a light on in the window and asked if they could snap a picture of me and my first truly big bass. Minus the catfish my fish weighed 6 ¾ pounds on a kitchen food scale! Best day? For me it ended perfectly, for the fish it was a trip to

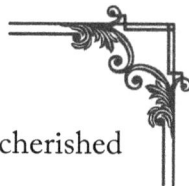

the taxidermist, which was customary in those days. A cherished memory of my first of many "best days."

A few more of a lifetime of best days would include a trip to Mexico all-expense paid by Bass Pro Shops as an outdoor writer and angler to get a story on a new lure in a remote Mexican lake. The lure, a Tornado a unique innovation of Louisiana native, Eugene "Shoe String" Dubois and was essentially a combination spinner and buzzbait.

After a day of air travel, we arrived in a small village on the shores of lake José Portillo. The next morning, we were motoring across the lake and after a short ride stopped in an innocent looking bay and proceeded to an area with a small point. Cast number one produced a bone jarring hit from a four-pound bass on a prototype of the newly invented lure. The next three hours were what every bass angler dreams of, 98 (yes, ninety-eight!) more bass ranging from 2 ½ to about 6 pounds hit that bait. My thumb was raw from landing those fish, and my triceps were cramping, and yes, we got pictures and all the inspiration we needed to generate publicity and interest in the new bait. We kept several fish to distribute to the poorest residents of the village. Best day? One of many to come.

On another trip I was invited to a lake development to do a promotional film for a firm hoping to sell high-end exclusive real estate inside the gates. We launched in a wild looking primitive lake with the entrance gained through a rust gate and a rough road. Armed with my constant companion, the jig, I looked at vast expanse of wild looking water—a steep bank, tons of standing trees, and cover everywhere. A drone, there to give an overhead film perspective, hovered over as I picked up the jig rod in hopes of hooking and landing a few fish for the film. I found myself in a massive school of bass. Cast after cast, it didn't even seem to matter where I pitched the bait, there was another bite. This unpressured lake gave up 62 bass in a little over two hours.

Invited to test out a 15-acre managed gated Tennessee lake, I gladly accepted the invitation. My first trip was more exploratory,

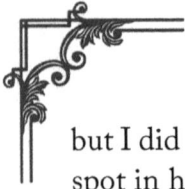

but I did catch a few decent bass and wrangled access to the same spot in hopes of catching what I believed might be some trophy fish. The next trip confirmed my suspicions as I landed several fish over five pounds, one a legitimate eight-pound largemouth. Late May, same lake, saw an early morning launch with intentions of a full day of fishing. Along for the ride was my light weight spinning outfit to test the waters for a few of the crappie and the huge bluegill that lived in this lake. I started with small, soft plastic tube, and each cast seemed to produce a hit—slab crappie and several giant hard fighting bluegills were eating nonstop. Enough of that foolishness—I reached for the bass baits and found a sweet spot loaded with largemouth! At day's end, as I locked the gate behind me, I had tallied up my catch 137 fish for the day, a bunch of crappie and bluegill but mostly BIG bass.

Another candidate for best day would have to be one of my farm pond trips. The pond, unbeknownst to the owner, had over the years become loaded with bass that rarely saw bait. In water stained by cattle wading the banks I managed to catch a few fish staged in a small mid-pond creek channel. It was late in the day when I picked up on an unusual situation. I was casting a topwater bait, and when I gave up on it getting bit I started a hasty retrieve back a solid three-pound bass aggressively just stopped the silver black back bait. Another cast using the stop and go method and this time a much bigger bass crushed the minnow plug. Then it became wild feeding spree as fish after fish couldn't resist my minnow imitating bait. At the end of the day I landed 17 bass with the five biggest estimated at close to over a 30-pound stringer. All released. The memory was the only keeper I needed.

Relegated to fishing after hours due to a strict work schedule, I often found myself casting after dark. Alone and under the stars I learned some valuable lessons about bass behavior. While many of these late night trips produced good numbers, a forever memory occurred as I fished a 9-inch black plastic worm across as spot named "the pump house point." Late into the evening (or early

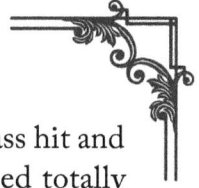

into the morning) I felt the now familiar *tap-tap* of a bass hit and leaned back on a respectable fish. Next the fish jumped totally silhouetted by the full moon and seemed to just hang in the air. This remains etched into my memory and made it one of my "best days"—or more correctly, best *nights*.

These and other days like them had several commonalities. A silent approach to the areas I fished, the use of quiet lures first, slightly stained to murky water color, cloud cover, just enough wind to create a ripple, often full or new moon, water temperatures in the high 50s to the mid 70s, and attention to retrieve speeds.

How about your best days? It's hard to recount those without smiling!

TROPHY TIP: In ultra-clear water consider fishing parallel to the bank and other edges. A cast to cover and a retrieve toward you brings a bass out and will often result in the fish literally seeing you as it approaches the bait. The eyesight of a bass below the surface is better than the eyesight of a human above the water. Remember, parallel edges, submerged wood, weed beds, docks or steep banks.

11

Getting Geared Up Equipment

The secret is simplicity and functionality! The four necessary functions of a fishing rod are these:

1. You should be able to comfortably be able to cast it accurately. Let's at least keep it in the same zip code
2. You should be able to feel everything the bait is doing regardless of the type of lure.
3. The rod should be capable of a solid hook set, using the proper technique. The correct amount of force depends on the angler.
4. You should be able to successfully play the fish all the way in.

Every rod of every type should fit these criteria. A few visual clues are cork handles (cork is more expensive), the number of rod guides (less than seven rid guides are scrimping on cost) and the material the rod is made of, because sensitivity and strength are biproducts of the material normally graphite.

Fishing Rods/Reels—Number one is my jig rod, it's a baitcasting model, always with me, and there are days I never put it down. Because it's my go-to, I demand light weight (this rod weighs about 4 ounces!), sensitive, and strong. One is the Lew's Custom Pro; the model number is TLCPSBR 6' 10". It's a medium heavy action rod with a line recommendation of 10 to 20-pound test and lures weighing ³⁄₁₆th to ⁵⁄₈th ounces. I ignore line recommendations because it could be one of three types of lines (monofilament,

fluorocarbon, braid). I use straight braid on my jig rod. I want a fast tip, and a rod heavier mid-section and stout in the butt section for a fast, sure hook set and the ability to play big fish in quickly. As far as lure weights I could but don't throw light weight lures (³⁄₁₆th) on my baitcasting gear. I opt for casting those on spinning equipment. My baitcasting reel continues the light weight theme, the Lew's custom light baitcasting reel (CLISH1) weighs less than six ounces and has a 7.5:1 retrieve ratio and capacity for 90 yards of line. This reel has the gears and the guts to stand up to lots of jigging, hard hook sets, and a drag that will control the big fish I'm looking for each time out.

For open face spinning equipment, a constant companion in the bait with me is the Mach 2 medium action spinning rod. (M266MS) This is for small light jig, smaller soft plastic (worms, curly tail grubs, tubes, ultra-light spinners (⅛th ounce) and small surface bait rod. I want a little flex in the tip and a strong butt section. This rod is 6'6" medium action, line recommended for this particular rod is 4 to 12-pound test and lures of ⅛th to a ½ ounce. I disagree with the recommendation. A ½ ounce lure is too heavy for this rod; that is more likely going to be on the baitcasting rig. My reel is either a Lew's Laser 50A or a Lew's Custom In Shore C1200 with a 6.2:1 retrieve ratio, a line capacity of 160 yards and pulling in 32 inches of line with each handle revolution. These are just a few of the rods I carry, but two that are always with me. Choosing rods and reels is a matter of preference but get equipment that fits you and your style(s) of fishing. I would avoid the new craze of blazing fast reels bragging about 10.1:1 retrieve ratios. It's easy to get caught up in the speed, but it is counter-productive in most situations.

THEORY: When fishing is tough, smaller lures and slower retrieves are the ticket to catching a few fish.

I have found it useful to get the reel handle cushions that slip

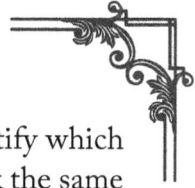

over the reel paddles, different colors allow me to identify which rod I want a quick glance. Redundant rods or reels look the same but could have different lures and uses and can become a little confusing at times.

There are a few outfits that I would describe as situational. For example, when the aquatic vegetation gets thick, I love throwing a hollow body frog (the Strike King KVD model). Because of the tangle of pads, moss, weeds, or grass this requires a heavy action rod, a reel capable of winching out a big bass from the heaviest cover and heavy, heavy braided line (40-pound test). This set up is of little use to me under other circumstance and is often left at home when conditions are not conducive, hence the descriptor "situational." If the crappie or bluegill bite, a whippy ultralight spinning combination will be on deck. The problem is if you accidentally hook a BIG bass, you're going to have an uphill battle getting it to the boat without getting your line and possibly your heart broken.

In the spring and early summer, I make it a habit to include the light spinning outfit to just do a little "junk fishing" (fishing for anything willing to bite) or to string a few fish for a fresh fish meal. For the serious trophy hunting angler, I would recommend one rod dedicated to casting crankbaits, spinners, and topwater plugs—a 7-foot medium action rod with a baitcasting reel geared at 6.3:1 for versatility. I would spool this reel with monofilament (12 or 14-lb. test Sufix Tritanium is my choice), and here's why. I want the rod to give a little in the tip to facilitate the hook set, and then once the fish is on, the rod goes when the fish runs and recovers when the fish is coming back toward the boat. I would also carry a 7-foot medium heavy action rod for backup as a jig/Texas rig soft plastic presentation rod. I would spool this with 20-lb. test monofilament. You could also use this rod as a big crankbait rod or for throwing the different chatter baits also know as a bladed jig.

THEORY: fishing line gets the least amount of attention in rank of importance. The line is like many people's car battery—until

it fails, it doesn't matter. Nothing could be further from the truth especially in the quest for truly big bass.

It's become popular to use "whippy" rods and braided line (listen for the line squeak on the fishing TV shows). The factor that allows for the limber rod is the use of braid which makes up for the lack of traditional stiffness in the fishing rod. The line and rod work in concert to create a solid hook set. The same rod set up with monofilament line would fail!

Line—For years this was easy. You could have monofilament or monofilament. The development of alterative fishing lines has been a great innovation, but it has created some misunderstanding about performance and the capabilities of each. Three basic choices are the old standby, monofilament, fluorocarbon, and braided lines.

- Monofilament—The unique quality about monofilament line is the stretch. Some of the authorities on such things report 10 to 15% stretch. This is good for some applications, in my opinion (spinnerbaits, crankbaits, and top water lures) Mono can be easily damaged in fishing around heavy cover, does offer different diameters, colors, and strengths, and even efficient knot strength. (More on knots later.) Mono does absorb a bit of water and needs to be changed out periodically. In my case at least every six months, maybe more often depending on use.

- Fluorocarbon—The rap against fluorocarbon for years was poor break strength. On the plus side flouro is virtually invisible in the water, has little to no stretch, and is a step up in sensitivity in comparison to monofilament. Another consideration is that it sinks slowly making it a poor choice for lighter topwater lures and some presentations. The use of fluorocarbon leaders has become wildly popular for use in conjunction with braided line on both spinning and baitcasting.

- Braided line—For years I shunned the use of braided lines

because of my previous success with monofilament and a fear that the constant use of braid would wear on the ceramic line guides on older fishing rods. There was also a problem with the waxy coating on the braid that would slip and cause loss of lure and largemouth. Line guides have been improved to accommodate the braided lines, and I have converted to widespread use of the braid in certain scenarios. I use darker colors, green or black braid for my jig rods, and NO leader. I want to tie directly to my braided lines. REASON: adding a leader adds an extra knot and increases the possibility of a failure. *See knots for an additional tip.

Knots—Keeping it simple and snug, I usually use only three knots: the Palomar, the clinch, and the blood knots. It's my contention that these three knots will serve you well in any technique/lure presentation. Rather than present a diagram, I suggest checking out a YouTube view of how-to in learning these knots. I have learned to trust the knot strength of both and would caution anyone that if you are not sure whether you trust the knot (of any kind) you've tied…RETIE it. I'd say more fish are lost because of poor knots or old line than any other reason.

When I tie on a jig or a Texas rig and in using braided line, I always use a double knot, first a Palomar and back it up with a clinch knot. This way even if the line were to slip, you would have snugged it up with the second knot. The blood knot is used to connect two lines, normally braid to fluorocarbon or other applications.

When spooling braided line on a spinning rod, I start with some older monofilament as a base to keep the braid from digging into itself. I run the monofilament to about 25% capacity of the reel spool. The mono cushions the braid, a blood knot connects the two and is trimmed closely as to not impede your smooth line flow on the cast. I add the braid to just short of capacity and then with another blood knot make a fluorocarbon leader about six inches shorter than my rod.

Other Items On board—I carry a floating pool thermometer

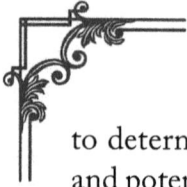

to determine surface temperature (critical in spawning, feeding, and potential location), a floating, rubberized landing net, dry box holding such essentials as my spare vehicle key, cell phone, first aid, pliers, small cutters for line, wire cutters to cut hooks in the event of an accident, sunglasses, hat. I also carry an accessories box, small cooler, head lamp for night fishing or late night emergencies. These are the minimum I carry. You can customize your own wants/needs.

TROPHY TIP: Check your rod guides for wear by passing a Q-tip through each eye, if any cotton is left you have a ragged spot that will eventually cut your line regardless to what type line you choose. As far as reels, a little lube on external parts throughout the year is generally adequate.

12

My Tackle Box

During my initial introduction to bass fishing I fell into the mental trap of thinking lots of lures made me a better fisherman. I soon realized this concept was an illusion that had me collecting baits that I saw, heard about, read about in magazine ads, or just looked like a good bet to help boat a bass. I still have 40-year-old artificial baits in the package that were either deemed too pretty to use or lost their appeal once I started catching bass on my list of the most reliable lures. In communicating to other anglers, I added a favorite restriction of mine to my presentations—the one-year rule. Essentially, it's this: you put anything you want in your tackle box, but if it doesn't get tied on, get wet, or catch a fish at the end of the year, you take it out. Same situation next year, and the following year. What you will find out is after a few seasons you'll have baits that you know work and a simplified system of selecting tackle while on the water.

I usually close this discussion with the statement that you already know what you're going to use. I never have and probably never will throw a jigging spoon. I don't like to Carolina rig. I rarely use a drop shot and don't own a glide bait.

In recapping previous success, especially for the true trophy fish, I determined that nearly 70% of my big bass came on soft plastics or jigs trailed with soft plastics. Plastic worms, craws, tubes, and creature-type baits rigged Texas rig, on leadheads or as jig trailers produce big bites and big bass. As a reminder this belief is based on criteria that are proven out each season. Natural or neutral colors, the most natural swimming or moving motions, bite sized baits and mostly silent. There are exceptions based on weather and water conditions, but these are the qualities that consistently draw the strikes I'm looking for in trophy fishing. My own system dictates the rod, reel, line, and presentations I use and have repeatedly experienced the most consistent big fish success day in and day out.

In the other compartments are a variety and a selection that I most believe in. I'm not a crankbait guy, but I have had some luck with cranking lures in certain situations. Crankbaits, shallow, deep, lipless, flat side, wide wobble, or otherwise earned a way into the trays. I should point out that there are seasonal baits that go in and out over the course of the year. For example, no top water lures when the water temperature is less than fifty. Jerkbaits are added for cold water and taken out once surface temps reach 60 degrees. While I love buzzbaits, and I've landed some genuine monsters on them, they leave in late fall and are replaced by modified single willowleaf blade spinnerbaits with shad-colored skirts. Speaking of spinners, I have a selection of blade types which include turtle shell, double willows for dirty water, Indiana for places that receive a lot of fishing pressure, and black blades for nighttime, BUT they all are ⅜th ounce models.

I think it's appropriate to describe the spinnerbait blades and their performance. Most often seen is the Colorado blade, for this reason I do shy away from using it. The Colorado is round and sends more vibration than any other blade, next the willowleaf which gives off the most flash and is so named because of the shape just like the leaf on a willow tree. The other I use is the Indiana blade which I would describe as tear-drop shaped. It's a blend of the other two in flash and the ability to produce vibration. The Indiana is a favorite because it's less used and gives the bass a different look and feel. There are other blades, but they are less often seen or used by manufacturers.

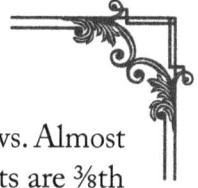

This brings me to a point that might raise some eyebrows. Almost exclusively my spinners, jigs, buzzers, and weighted baits are ⅜th ounce versions. I put a premium on casting accuracy, and the feel of the lure is a big part of that mindset for me. If everything I pick up weighs the same, it positions me to place the bait exactly where I want without interruption because I changed bait types.

Other must-have lures are minnow imitators and squarebill crankbaits, two sizes, three colors. Colors I choose and use are based off water color, sky color, and wind velocity. Each of these factors will determine the light penetration in the water. Because bass are sight feeders this detail has proven over the years to be critical in color selection. Clear water, clear sky, minimal wind = neutral color like a shad color; stained water, cloudy, and a significant wind ripple means I'm going with a crawfish pattern. In muddy water, dark skies, and significant wind which gives a minimal amount of light penetration it's a bold color like chartreuse/black back, fire, tiger orange belly, or red.

For my beloved buzzbaits skirt, color choices are similar to the crankbait criteria with one exception—the amount of wind or velocity will determine the size of my blade. As a rule, I believe the big blade draws strike from the bigger fish, but I use smaller blades when the water is calm or clear, medium size for the in-between times, and mega blades for high wind and dirty water.

During prime top water time, if I'm not throwing a buzzer (I'll still have one tied on) I'll have multiple lures that have drawn big hits from good size bass. A surface minnow imitator is a forgotten bait among all the glitz and glitter of the current lures. The most popular color pattern for years has been the silver/black back. Old timers presentation, cast out and let it sit until all the ripples disappear, (seriously) give it a few small twitches, this is often when it gets eaten, rest (count seven), twitch, rest, repeat back to the boat. This is tough to do because we have migrated to a run-and-gun style of fishing. The dog walking baits, cup faced poppers, frog baits, and other surface lures require a cadence that may change depending on the feeding mood of the bass. It needs to look injured or in flight mode. The only way to figure it out is to experiment but almost always slower is better. Start slow and ramp up.

I also save tray space for Texas rig accessories. Sinkers ⅛th ounce up to ½ ounce, hooks, 3/0, 4/0, and 6/0 and red beads. Texas rig is first on the line thread on a slip sinker, most common for me is the ⅜th ounce, I then add a red bead. The bead adds a color, a clicking sound as the sinker claps against the bead, and also serves to protect you knot. Lastly is the worm-style hook. I use a jig-style hook with a small spring-like device clipped to the eye of the hook to get a straight hang on my plastic bait. I normally carry a 4/0 hook for straight shaped plastics (worms) a 6/0 hook for bigger flipping tube baits.

I carry small accessory type boxes for quick access to accommodate more jig choices, seasonal crankbaits sorted by color, diving capacity, and water temperature. The jigs might be finesse jigs (clear water), hair jigs (cooler water), lighter or dark for various water colors, heavier for windy days, and some identical to my personal favorites as spares.

The smaller cranking boxes are interchangeable: lipless go in the late winter/early spring, the flat side deeper diving for cool water conditions and squarebills for heavy cover. Because the squarebills are frequently run into the gnarly cover I carry two of each of my favorite colors.

These are a list of my basic baits, but I can tell you I've been with a few great fishermen who had one strange quirk about them. They in some cases, carried a bare minimum of tackle! My friend Mike toted a bag of generic soft plastic craws in one crawfish color, two rods, a couple of hooks and sinkers, that was it. He caught a bunch of bass! Another angling acquaintance, Jerry, wore a floppy golf hat and brought one spinning rod and several 2/0 live bait style hooks imbedded in the band of his hat—that's all. When we went fishing, he would walk the banks, and whatever

live creature he could catch he would use for bait. He seldom got skunked! My friend Michael lives to throw a big soft plastic frog with paddle-style feet. The frog is black with white feet, and he goes through about 300 a year and catches bass everywhere and almost year-round using that frog.

In closing, recognize that we all have favorites baits and styles. When I first started, I wanted to pick one style of fishing and become an expert at it. I'm still trying to achieve that status, but my strength is definitely feel-bait fishing, soft plastic baits of every kind, size, color, and shape, or bass jigs.

TROPHY TIP: Work to learn new techniques and lure presentations for the toughest days. Give a new bait 30 minutes and then go back to one of your favored baits or techniques. 10 casts aren't going to teach you much; give each a legitimate shot. This does require self-discipline, and it's all part of becoming a complete fisherman and being able to catch bass consistently.

13

Common Mistakes

Often when speaking in public, one quote I have used is, "Everyone makes mistakes, that's why they put erasers on the back of pencils." In fishing I've made every mistake possible, and it has frequently cost me big bass. It's my contention you can't make many mistakes and catch a big fish. I've lost fish in every way imaginable, some that make you lose sleep at night, genuine giants. Learning from the mistake and trying to eliminate that possibility is the path to continuous improvement in any venture, including fishing. Eliminating errors positions you to becoming more proficient at fooling and landing the biggest bass. Here are some of the problems I experienced.

Early on I fell into the trap of trusting whatever I heard. On the advice of an old timer I started using a snap swivel to attach my lures to the line. You don't have to retie, you can make a quick bait switch, the lure moves more freely—it all seemed like a good idea, until…I hooked a big bass, and it bent the wire on the swivel allowing it to get off. I've never trusted a swivel since. The major take-away from this experience—any time you add a component you create a potential failure point.

While employing a minimalist approach, there are times for some form of redundancy. I once busted a propeller on a trolling motor. It was the primary source of movement in my flat bottom boat. Simple solution: carry a spare. You can't bring a spare of everything, but you can carry critical items—a spool of line, a matching favorite bait, vehicle keys, and more. I also bring an additional life jacket in my truck and a small collapsible paddle when kayaking. No one wants to be up the creek without a…yeah, *paddle*.

A common error is not recognizing a pattern. In any type of fishing, patterns emerge, but you must apply a sense of awareness. How deep was the first fish? What bait did it hit? How fast/slow was your retrieve? What type of cover was around? All these and more create the ability to repeat the success of the catch by recognizing the pattern. If you don't, it can make for a long day. When you quickly discern a pattern, you may pull the biggest string of bass ever. Be aware that a pattern can change because of clouds moving in (or out), position of the sun, rain, wind, or even boating activity.

How about reading water? Because I don't rely on electronics, I use visual clues to assist in locating and catching fish. An incoming creek to me spells increased oxygen (critical in the summer months), a large bare spot on a hillside probably indicates what I refer to as a *slide* where a tree fell and cleared a path down to the water. Somewhere there's a partially or fully submerged tree. In moving water, finding a current break, maybe a bridge piling, a point, rock, a tree a dock—any of these creates a hideout for a fish avoiding, *but using*, the current to deliver food sources. A steep bank will continue to be steep in the water. This offers a clue as to the depth you could be casting your bait into. Shade created by a dock, an overhanging tree, or anything else is likely to harbor at least one fish, maybe a giant seeking color water and an ambush point. Don't let electronics rob you of your observation skills and use of common sense.

Technical Difficulties—Here's a list of some common difficulties. If you're in a hurry to tie a knot, you could be making a mistake, and if your line breaks at your poorly tied knot, you can lose bait AND bass. Not moistening the line as you tighten it down creates heat, and this is the worst thing for your monofilament or fluorocarbon lines. Is your drag set properly? I set mine by the

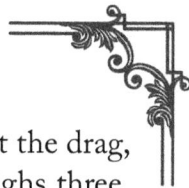

experience of feel, but if you want a standard way to set the drag, use about a three-pound weight, or anything that weighs three pounds to ensure your drag will slip under the pull of a larger fish. Too loose and you can't control the fish, too tight and the biggest of the fish might break your line—neither adds up to a grip and grin photo.

Another valuable tip is when you have several days between trips, to ensure your drag will slip under the weight of a heavy fish, before the first cast place your thumb across the spool of a baitcasting reel tightly and give the handle a quarter turn forward to free up the drag system. For spinning reel grab the front of the spool and give a gentle turn counter-clockwise to accomplish the same thing with your open face spinning reel. Not keeping your hooks sharp is another potential error. Even freshly broken out of the packaging, I check continuously on the sharpness of my hooks. I'm so paranoid about sharpness I keep a diamond file hook sharpener in my pocket! Points can become dull from use, dragging through rocks, sticking on submerged wood, and coming into contact with heavy cover. I want my hooks sticky-sharp where they catch on your fingernail when dragged across.

Not replacing old or heavily used fishing line with a fresh spooling is a problem. Change your line out often especially if you fish often or around heavy cover. In doubt? I also repeatedly check the first few feet of my line while fishing to make sure the knot looks good and there are no frays. Go through the list and make corrections before it costs you the fish of a lifetime.

While I am a fan of covering a lot of water, in some cases (rarely for me) people will sit on a fishing hole. I call it camping out. Occasionally in a deep-water situation this might pay off. There could be a school of bass that might get fired up, and you might pull three or more from the school. But I believe that most of the time if there is a big fish in area, it will hit first. That bigger fish is often a loner, and I refer to these places as a one-fish-spot.

I believe the use of the newer electronics may very well change

bass behavior. Fishing for electronically visible bass may very well send them deeper or back to the banks. Time will tell.

In playing fish, first in hooking and landing BIG bass, you should be mentally prepared for seeing a giant jump or the drag screaming after setting the hook on that giant. Don't panic! Don't try to bring a big one in too fast, this is especially true with a trophy smallmouth. Regardless of species if the fish is too green let the equipment (rod and reel) do the work. Drag set, rod back, and steady pressure are all vital. I do try to land fish as quickly as possible but not force it. Steady pressure on the fish by keeping the rod tip back makes the bass work against the equipment and the rod doing exactly what it was designed to do. Another tactic when playing a fish is push the front of the rod down into the water for two reasons, it's less likely to jump and then the fish is working against water pressure as opposed to air pressure.

Blind casting—This is just randomly casting without recognition of a specific reason to target an area with your bait. Be deliberate and open to determining a pattern that may be emerging or changing due to weather, wind, cloud cover, losing sunlight, a different type of bank, cover, or bottom contour.

Another valuable tip is to cast past the target, not right to it. A scat to a dock or stump or another potential fish-holding object is likely to spook the bass. Launch your lure past the holding area and bring it past giving the predatory fish a limited view or less time to scrutinize the lure. Remember, you're trying to fool a fish into believing that your bait is a food source that made the mistake of venturing too close or is injured or trying to escape.

Look at the plastic lip of your crankbaits often to make sure they aren't cracked or chipped because that will change the performance of the bait. They can only be bounced off hard objects and even the surface so many times until they are damaged. Watch the front hole of your buzzbait blade also, it too will eventually become damaged or broken from wear (and hopefully fish) and will start *limping* along on the retrieve. Carry spares of your favorites.

Land 'Em Or Lose 'Em—Ever had a big one break your line? It could be weak line, a nick in your line, or a poorly tied knot. On the ever-popular braid, I start with a Palomar knot backed up by a clinch knot just in case the braided line slips. Another critical factor is a needle sharp hook. A properly set drag is important when you have that Big un' on the end of your line also. While some tournaments do not allow nets, I keep one well within reach when I'm in BIG bass territory. Developing an effective hook set is also on the list. For spinnerbaits, crankbaits, and topwater lures I employ a sweeping hook set, for jigs, plastic worms, and other soft plastics I try to cross their eyes with an over-the-shoulder hard snap of the rod. Keep in mind a truly BIG bass has most likely been hooked before and will try to get into heavy cover. Have each aspect of your equipment stout enough to winch them out.

A tactic that might help you catch fish and *not* lose your lures when fishing a submerged tree, if I'm going to parallel the tree with my bait, I fish in the direction from the trunk to tree top. This reduces the chance of getting stuck in the branches. Your bait Is running with the branches, *not* into the V created by the branches.

TROPY TIP: Keep constant contact with all your baits. Most anglers focus on the jig and plastic worm, but a bass can inhale a crankbait or spinnerbait, and you may never feel the big hit. When a fish is coming toward you it might be just a *different* feel because of slack in the line. Any tine you feel anything different, set the hook...it's free! Don't be lulled into a halfhearted hook set, hit them like it's the biggest bass of your life. It might just be!

14

Fishing The Feel Baits

My records show a majority of my fish over five pounds came on what I refer to as *feel type* baits, soft plastic or jigging baits moved with the rod. Crankbaits and spinnerbaits are examples of the baits moved with the reel. There's so much more to say about lures in this category, you could probably write a book about just this topic. One observation is that if you were bass fishing in the '70s and '80s you probably had a fiberglass rod and monofilament line. This set up would eventually teach you lessons that would make you a great *worm fisherman*. The point being if you could feel them, set the hook, play them, and land them on this less than ideal gear it's a cinch with the new technology and materials used for rods, reels, and lines, to successfully catch bass on soft plastics now.

Because my first few big bass were caught on a jigs and plastic worms, I tend to favor this category of artificial lures. I also dedicated myself to becoming as adept as I could at one type of lure and then learning as much as I could about other baits and styles. I found that I always returned to the feel baits. This area is where my confidence lies, and I have, season after season, had the most success for genuine giant size bass.

Let's start with the technical side of equipment. Early on I was forced to just use what I had, there was no worm rod, cranking rod, or spinnerbait rod, just the *only* rod I had. With a young family my fishing equipment was bare bones, and one spincasting rod

was a multipurpose. After losing several fish because I couldn't get a solid hook set, I finally acquired a pistol grip, stiff as a pool cue worm rod. It was even designated on the shaft as a *worm rod*. Still forced to use the spincast reel because of cost, I eventually had to replace my push button reel with the reel described as a *level wind baitcasting* model, the quality and power were a must for what I wanted to accomplish. After hundreds of backlashes and many spools of line, I reached an acceptable level of proficiency, more and more bass came to the boat, and I felt like I was always ready for the big bite.

Many rods later (many, many), I've refined my jig/worm gear. There are many manufacturers that offer high quality rods and reels. I've come to depend on the Lew's line up of equipment. It's my belief the rod choice should personally fit the angler. I'm 5 foot 10 and need a 7 ½ foot rod to cast and work reasonably. I prefer a medium heavy action rod with fast tip and extremely strong butt section. A smaller or taller person might need a different set up. The rod should fit you. The whole point is to be able to cast, feel ,and achieve a consistently efficient hook set and then to play the biggest bass in—see four functions of a fishing rod in Chapter 11. My jig or worm rod weighs about five ounces.

As for the reel, I want something that will winch a big bass out of the ugliest cover and along with the rod allow me to control any fish. Also having the correct reel, the proper line, and drag set all work in unison to accomplish this. A low-profile baitcasting reel fits my hand comfortably, and I prefer a midlevel retrieve gear ratio as to not get lulled into fishing the bait in too quickly—the 6.8:1 ratio is my preference. My reels usually weigh less than 6 ounces meaning my rod and reel together weighs around 11 ounces. This outfit allows me to fish comfortably for hours.

Aside from the comfort level physically and mentally, the qualities of the rod are vital. The rod length helps to determine casting distance and accuracy, assist in taking up the slack, setting the hook, playing the fish, and wearing them down. When you find the right

system for you, it becomes an extension of you. This is another area where I have an identical or redundant rig in the event I need one.

My line is straight braid, normally 25 pound, no more than 40 pound test with no leader. Some folks opt for a leader for fear that a fish will see the line. I can't discount that possibility, but I believe a properly presented bait of any kind has the fish so committed that it is zeroed in on the lure. Exceptions are ultra-clear water ,at which time I will attach a fluorocarbon leader or use a permanent marker to color 2 or 3 inches of the first 12 feet of my line incrementally making the line break up in the sight line of the fish. For many years I was relegated to the use of heavy monofilament line, and the advent and improvement of the braids eventually won me over. I do double knot my braided line with the first knot being a Palomar backed up by a clinch knot, this combination gives me the confidence that the knot won't be a point of failure, that the bait and the bass are secure.

The ability to tell what the bait is doing at all times is critical to this style of fishing. The proper line and rod work in concert to transmit the swim, tick of cover, the bass inhaling the lure all the time. This brings us to the weight of the bait. The bait details are a matter of preference, but foremost the ability to accurately cast the lure is partially dependent on the weight. A finesse jig or light slip sinker could make it hard to place the bait into that sweet spot where you believe the bass is holdup. The weight also has a bearing on the descent or fall of the bait—vital when the bite is tough or the conditions extreme. Cold or hot water will slow the metabolism down of bass of all sizes, so keeping the bait on the strike zone is easier with the lighter weight lure. Light is relative, I'm always equipped with jigs and lead in the ⅛th ounce class and up to ¾th of an ounce. The heavier one is a last resort in heavy wind or when punching through the thickest vegetation or cover. The weight is important in allowing the angler full contact with the lure at all times. My consistent choice and the best results have been achieved for me with the middle of the road size ⅜th ounces.

The Color Controversy—Whatever you have the most confidence in is the bait color you're going to use; no one will convince you of anything else. As with other baits, my choices are dictated by several criteria. Water color, sky color, and wind velocity are all factors as to the amount of light that penetrates the water. The light penetration is key because of the sight feeding habits of the bass. The lure choice is based off the food source you are trying to imitate, and without question your positive experiences are all part of the decision as to what color you will tie on. Brightly colored baits do catch bass, but it's my belief that more natural and neutral colors are the ones bitten regularly by the big bruisers! Pumpkin, brown, white, shad, and different shades of natural craw patterns all deserve a chance to fool a big fish. Don't rule out straight black and not just for night use, I've found it to be good in dirty water and in the winter. Purple seems to be ageless, and the combination of blue and red produces purple. A slight hint of another shade or a muted highlight can also be effective. Years ago, I would customize colors by laying plastics strategically together to allow them to bleed into each other.

Once you've settled on your bait you can merely cast, flip, or pitch it.

CASTING is the most common method, and once your bait lands, allow it to fall straight while still keeping in touch to some degree with the bait. If you immediately engage the reel, the bait will automatically arc back, and you are missing a major portion of the strike zone, if you can allow the bait to descend with a minimum of slack you get a great vertical view for the bass. Once the reel is engaged, begin the return retrieve using a swimming, hopping, resting return. There are dozens of variations to this, and this is the random action so important and deadly for fooling bass. Some folks let the bait just sit on the bottom (dead sticking), others do a slow drag, and still other will keep the bait in motion. I visualize the natural (there's that word again) movement of a crawfish or swimming minnow, shad, or snake.

As far as flipping, you can thank the pros and media for the confusion of flipping in reference to pitching, they're *different* presentations.

FLIPPING is a technique developed on the West Coast and essentially is using a limited amount of line, probably 6 to 9 feet, and a pendulum motion for a close-range presentation, normally positioned around 4 to 12 feet from various types of heavy cover.

PITCHING is far and away my favorite for many reasons. You can keep a more preferred distance from your target and less risk of spooking a big bass. I routinely pitch from a range of 10 to 30 feet. Another plus, when properly executed the bait travels just above the water's surface and silently, just barely, *dimples* the water as it enters. Depress the thumbar on the baitcasting reel with about enough line to be even with the reel, start the rod forward letting the rod take the bait from your hand, *feather* the spool with a hint of pressure, just as you would with a cast, controlling the distance. In pitching the rod gives the bait direction; your *educated* thumb gives distance. Point the rod directly at you target and release the lure with a smooth forward flow. This is a huge factor in my success at catching trophy size bass. Practice and perfect this presentation—you'll be glad you did.

I recommend three-point contact when feel bait fishing as opposed to the traditional two points. First point of contact is the rod tip, next the handle, and an additional contact point can be the fishing line resting on the back of your thumb. The back part of your thumb is sensitive and gives a subtle sensation when the line is picked up by the fish. As you work the bait back to you, make sure not to bring the rod back to past what would best be described as the 10 o'clock position. This allows you to lower the rod quickly when you feel a hit, pick up, or strike. If you raise the rod straight up to 12 o'clock you will frequently find yourself out of position to perform a good hook set. Another suggestion is to keep a loose grip on the rod to allow a better feel coming from the handle to alert you to any end of the line activity. A tight death grip on the rod handle numbs the feel.

The Moment of Truth—"There one!" These are the frequently uttered words once you sense an interruption in the trip back to the boat; a strike! In analyzing the strike, the fish inhales or grabs the bait, that in turn sends a message transmitted through the rod to your hands and then to the brain. The automatic response should be to lower the rod slightly, leaving a bit of slack line, bend at the knees and with a super quick motion bring the rod back past your head driving the hook home. You lower the rod to utilize the slack as you would when driving a nail. You wouldn't place the hammer directly on the nail, you pull back leaving a gap and then slam the hammer. This hook set is reversing the process with the same result—a solid, powerful, and effective outcome. Bending at the knees allows you to generate additional leg power as athletes do in other sports (golf, basketball, baseball). Properly executed, you put 11 pounds of pressure on the hook point on the hook set, that'll drive it through any part of a bass.

If you're fishing the Texas rig with a lead slip sinker and you feel like you missed a bite, take a close look at the lead sinker...it will literally have tooth marks on it similar to the striation marks on a fired bullet, the lead dulls and oxidizes so when it's scraped it show the bright shine of fresh lead under dulled color.

Playing a feel bait hooked fish is much the same as other baits, keep steady pressure on the fish. It does seem the fish hooked well below the surface often rocket through the water, jump, and do the classic head shakes trying to dislodge the lure. If you've followed the steps to the hook set, there's no need to repeat the process. Often anglers, not trusting their initial set, slam the fish repeatedly. Salt water angers do this, I believe, because of the inordinate amount of line they have between them and the ocean fish. This actually could make the hook penetration spot larger and allow the fish to escape by easily throwing the bait. Always control the fish by using the rod, steady pressure, and a properly set drag.

In the toughest of conditions, I will take a finesse jig, a ¼ or even ⅛th ounce and add a full-size soft plastic craw to create an

agonizingly slow fall. In the right place at the right time bass can't resist this presentation. Wacky or floating worm rigs fished weightless also are slow fall presentations for the angler patient enough to employ them.

TROPHY TIP: If you're truly trophy hunting, don't be afraid to tie on a big (long) plastic worm or another large, soft plastic lure. Big baits do catch big bass, and at night it's even better. Use enough weight, minimally a ⅜th ounce slip sinker and a sharp quality hook that allows you to get the best hook set. Carry a few 5/0 and 6/0 worm hooks for those big *snakes*.

15

That Strike Zone

The size of the bass' strike zone, in my opinion, has been misrepresented for years. Folks talk about a bass rocketing across the lake 50 feet to hit a bait—it makes no sense. Not to say it's impossible, but let's say very unlikely. Simply stated the amount of energy expended by a fish to do a long-distance chase means it wouldn't receive an equal or greater amount of nutritional value than it spent. In this case the bass gets *smaller* instead of larger. If you think about it, this why short-range techniques (flipping or pitching) or casts into the home territory of bass get hammered sometimes almost immediately. I like to refer to this as making a house call. BIG bass don't get big by long distance chases; they get big by taking advantage of opportunistic occurrences and by staking claim to the prime areas that best serve their needs.

I was so excited to get an underwater affirmation watching a televised major tournament where the camera followed a Forward Facing Sonar view showing a big bass following a tournament angler's lure from a big submerged tree in 25 feet of water. The bass *tracked* the lure for several feet and then gave up because what I believe was the distance or the speed of the lure dissuaded the bass from biting. Once the fish gave up it immediately returned to the tree it emerged from.

If there's oxygen, food, and cover they'll claim their territory. In the best areas, they stay until the food sources dry up, otherwise there's no reason to leave. This explains why certain spots seem to consistently hold bigger bass season after season. We have a place on my home lake known as the *double digit bank*, it earned that name because several fish over ten pounds have come from that very specific stretch of the lake. Another aspect of the new technology is it just further proves my theory of presenting baits to a specific target for best success. The new age techno anglers find the fish and then pitch soft plastics using the very same tactic I've employed for years, slow moving, silent baits with a natural motion and random action.

Armed with the knowledge of where a bass lives, it is highly desirable to work proven places every time on the water. It's also beneficial to use baits and presentations that keep the bait in the face of the fish for an extended period of time. Slow falling lures, suspending lures like a jerkbait, and others will test the resolve of even the most lethargic bass. The pause, hesitation, or stop teases the bass into a closer scrutiny and often into eating the slow-moving creature that has invaded its territory.

Last season during the fall we were exploring a stretch of the Elk River that is the headwaters for our home lake. With little knowledge of the river, I used my extensive previous river experiences to take me to the most fishy looking spots. We gravitated to points, current breaks, green aquatic vegetation, and of course the biggest submerged trees available. I had positioned myself in the middle of a huge fallen oak tree located in about seven feet of water and began pitching a jig to every opening, gliding through and around the trunk, branches, and the tree top pointing out to the main river channel when…I felt a gentle steady pressure (aka resistance) and a swimming motion into the main tree trunk. In my experience all those details are generally the signs of a heavy-weight bass inhaling your bait. Too slow! The fish spit my jig and left me with the thought of, *I wonder how big that bass was?* After mentally marking the exact spot I made a silent vow to return soon.

On the next major moon, full I believe, I was methodically

working a big Texas rigged worm in the same area, strike two, and I missed again, this time not recognizing the hit because the wind was pushing me around, and the bass was swimming with the bait towards me. More determined now than ever, I planned to come back after letting the area and bass rest. About ten days later I plotted my revenge against the elusive Elk River fish. Reverting back to my memory bank, I remember wacky rigging soft plastic straight stick type worms. I re-rigged a spinning rod with a fast tip and a lot of backbone. I changed out the monofilament line to 20-pound test braid and added a five-foot section of six-pound test fluorocarbon for the invisible, no stretch qualities I thought might tilt the odds in my favor. An additional adjustment was the use of a 3/0 circle hook—a deadly detail when dealing with lure shy fish. Once you sense a bite and using the circle hook you merely start to reel (no hook set), and the hook slides up inside the mouth of the fish and anchors in the side of the mouth. The circle hook is incredibly efficient and works with other artificial baits as well as live bait.

Believing that the fish that had already bested me two previous times was a resident fish I started to cruise through the general vicinity and work any cover and certainly the submerged wood where I had my previous encounters. There, a lone tree top had been pushed gently to create a current break in about six feet of water, and I eased up to it. Rigged and ready I used an underhand pitch to deliver the watermelon/red flake worm to the upstream side of the tree, watched as it drifted, and gave it gentle twitches to allow my soft plastic lure to navigate through the limbs. As the bait slowly dropped into a few smaller branches the line took on a different feel. As I pulled up gently, I felt an undeniable pressure and began reeling, the circle hook did exactly what it was supposed to do and almost immediately the bass tried to reenter the protection of the submerged tree. I coaxed the fish toward the middle of the river and open water and played my prize into my grip. There was my bass, 6 ½ pounds of largemouth. After a few quick pictures a gentle release into the stained river waters followed.

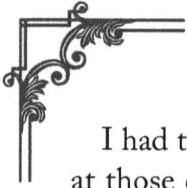

I had thrown spinnerbaits, squarebill crankbaits and buzzbaits at those exact same spots in previous trips. Lessons learned or maybe reinforced, this fish had staked out this area because of an abundant food supply, shad, bluegill, and crawfish. The heavy cover was its sanctuary, and the ideal depth was somewhere between four and eight feet. Also not lost on me was that while the three bites I got were on different baits, they were all of the family of feel baits!

There are examples of hot spots; deep zones that hold bass. There exists a legion of ledge fishermen working deep water drop offs in many of the river system lakes especially during the summer months. I have fired up schooling fish running crankbaits through them but have seldom caught anything bigger than four-pound bass in these situations. Others have had success doing this, but I believe pulling a giant bass out is less likely in extremely deep water. The deepest I've ever caught any bass was 23 feet, the deepest BIG bass was on a bluff bank and 15 feet of water. The newest electronics allow anglers to find and watch fish as the lure is presented—still no guarantee that they'll bite.

THEORY: Bass in shallow water are there throughout their lives for two reasons, 1. To spawn. 2. To feed. In spawning the shallow water is necessary for the incubation of the eggs. Immediately after the spawn bass, will generally move to deeper water, rest, and then return (shallow) to feed and regain their strength.

For seasons in my journals, I made notations about every detail of each BIG bass catch. My notes included water color, wind direction, moon phases, water levels (stable, falling, or rising) surface water temperature, cover that held the bass, lure used, and even retrieve speed if I felt it was relevant.

If you have watched some of the new style tournaments, you see bass anglers trying to catch the most fish, the most weight as individuals or teams. Watch closely as what are believed to be the best in the business almost without exception on unfamiliar waters

ignore electronics and move to shorelines, marinas, and boat docks to quickly catch their fish. The magic waters seem to be eight feet or less, and any different cover is where the catches occur. Coincidence, or proof of my findings? With people employing multiple screens and high-tech electronics, it's turned into a video game. Still I predict bass of all sizes will abandon the deep brushpiles and out of survival relocate to deeper sanctuaries or the heaviest cover they can find, it's a cyclical story. All this being said, keep in mind truly BIG bass are a different creature. Much like an old whitetail, once they reach 4 or 5 years old and their instincts and survival experiences are ingrained, they seem to disappear or are only taken during the rut, just like a bass being more susceptible when they are spawning.

Besides depth another clue for me is the surrounding area. If there's an abundance of rock I would think there are crawfish, so a jig or a Texas rigged craw would be on one of my rods. Shallow shore line vegetation would support bluegill, minnows, and potentially frogs, and once more mimicking these natural foods in conjunction with the immediate surroundings would make sense and position you to fool the biggest fish in that spot. In any zone, locate secondary cover, I've seen this repeatedly produce trophy fish. Another plus is when water levels are dropping due to weather or the winter draw down, the *secondary* cover becomes the *primary* cover.

Strike Zone Lesson: It was mid-March, and I was fishing my home lake; the surface water temperature was 58 degrees, and we were three days off the full moon. There was a fair amount of big boat pressure as the tournament season had started. I was fishing an area that I had become familiar with in the last year and moved to a steep bank with an abundance of rock and submerged wood. A slight tail wind had my kayak drifting, and I was pitching to visible targets. The wind drift can make certain retrieves a little more difficult to control. Sitting in around 8 feet of water, I felt resistance and *chalked it up* to being a piece of wood on the bottom,

but something just didn't seem right, so I put my jig back in exactly the same spot and felt a constant tug. My immediate response is to set the hook, and when I did my rod bowed over to the weight of a good size bass. A fight punctuated with three jumps and a legit eight pounder was in my grip. From this experience I learned (or reinforced in my mind) the silence of the kayak is deadly, the strike zone can be tiny, and that the same fish had been fooled *twice* in less than 30 seconds by the slow presentation of the jig.

THEORY: With any fluctuation of weather or some water conditions I believe the bigger bass soon relocate to the next available cover. Secondary wood, a stump, submerged tree, an off-shore weed bed, a hump or depression, a creek channel, or a combination of these factors produce BIG bites. Any other potential food sources also will seek a stopping point or shelter in secondary isolated cover which sets up a perfect ambush scenario. Bugs, snakes, frogs, birds, other fish all fall into this category of creatures seeking a rest stop that could be a fatal error and turn them into fish food.

TROPHY TIP: If possible, stand while fishing your jigs, worms and soft plastics. Standing gives you much more leverage, a huge advantage on the hook set and more control over playing your big fish. *Life jackets 100% of the time.

16

New Water

My style is radically different than many people and even those I fish with. I return repeatedly to an area that I can cover in one day and pick the place apart, becoming intimately familiar with ever aspect of a cove, shoreline, pocket, or pool. Most people become bored with one particular launch or even body of water. While I don't sit still, I may cover a prospective spot repeatedly especially if it has BIG bass potential or after I score a trophy. With any degree of success, I make a mental note of exactly what happened for future reference. The goal for me always is a predictable bite, and if I pull a few BIG bass from an area you can bet, I'll be back...often!

When approaching new water for various reasons I apply the same logic each time. I go with my strengths as far as techniques, tackle, and lure choices, then quite simply I look for water that as closely as possible matches where I have had past successes. Stumped still? Go to shoreline cover, irregular banks transitioning from mud to rock, gravel to weed cover, points, steep shorelines with fallen trees, boat docks, bridge pilings, or corners in coves.

Years back I made a trip to a Canadian wilderness area known as the *Quetico*, three million square acres of wild country with a third of it being water. So I'm hundreds of miles from home staring at tannic stained water resembling weak iced tea, some places literally 100 feet deep. Wild waters, glacier lakes teeming with fish,

lake trout, walleye, northern pike, and smallmouth bass—thousands of smallmouths. Certainly, new water. Where do you start? There were native minnows, brown and gold in color, crawfish, a shad look-alike, and a smaller shiny baitfish. A self-proclaimed shallow water fisherman, I ruled out multi-hook lures because of the never-give-up, thrashing fight of the smallmouth and my lack of interest in trying to dig hooks out of my hands. One rod had a double Colorado bladed spinnerbait; the other a medium size buzzbait. Working my way through a large bay I launched a cast with a hope and prayer to some off-shore big boulder rock, and my spinnerbait came to screeching halt followed by my drag giving line grudgingly, and a smallmouth taking flight five times in the next 30 seconds. Good guess OR calculated game plan? Late that day I found a few downed cedar trees and ran a buzzbait past the naked branches and watched as a big brown shadow emerged from the shadows and crushed the buzzer. Both bait decisions were based off past success in smallmouth waters in my home state of Tennessee. Different waters, same fish!

After years of fishing lakes in Missouri, I relocated to Tennessee and found a home across the road from a small river. New water, moving water, loaded with wood, aquatic vegetation, *and* fish. Hard to access and receiving limited fish pressure, the river became a test tank for me. The lake lures I had become accustomed to weren't as well received in this spot. I began experimenting with the jig, the bait that had produced my biggest bass to date. What happened next was the stuff dreams are made of. Apparently, these wild bass had never seen a jig and old pork frog combo commonly known as a *jig and pig*. For the next twenty years I had a secret location and found these fish more than willing to hit a well-placed, jig, buzzbait, plastic worm, or a number of other lures. I learned big lessons on a small body of water that would also apply to larger lakes.

Doing TV for years, I was challenged to go to various locations to film and catch fish on camera. This was all new water. We never failed to film a catch, mostly because I applied the familiar water

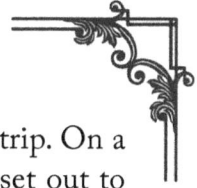

logic to the untested places we launched into on each trip. On a midsize public lake in the middle of the summer we set out to test the *can you catch a big bass on new waters* question. We were challenged to quickly (we usually had about a total of five hours to film) find and land a few fish on totally unfamiliar waters with the caveat of making it a trophy size bass as an additional challenge. Launching a full-size bass boat into a state managed public lake, I scanned the area looking for something that might hold promise and a BIG bass. True to form I never even flipped the switch on the available electronics. With four rods rigged and on the deck, I dropped the trolling motor and started down a bank that had a topwater look to it. Working irregular shorelines punctuated by the occasional fallen tree, some weedy spots or a few big rocks jutting out into the water, and nothing. The slow troll and a topwater plug didn't produced, and I began to formulate a new game plan. Spotting a few brush piles and big submerged trees I made may way over to the wood evidenced by the branches poking through the surface. One particular area was located maybe 15 feet off on a point. Wood and a point—two potential attractions. Pitching a Texas rigged large bass tube and working it through the branches, it ticked and swam when I saw a flash and felt a hit. I announced to the cameraman I had a bite, he took a moment to get me in focus, and by then the bass had rejected the bait. Next up, the buzzbait in a section of stumps. I worked the buzzer over and around the stumps using all the tricks I knew to try to draw a hit; nothing.

Taking a brief break to down a bottle of water, I spied in the distance another point with a giant submerged tree paralleling the point in what looked like a spot where the lake had a slowly tapering bottom going from a few feet to about ten feet. I looked into the camera and said out loud, "A long point, ten feet of water, and a big tree—there's bound to be a bass in there." I confess said this with more hope than conviction.

Knowing it created a feel for running a crankbait down the wood and across the branches was risky, I decided on a *baby bass*

patten plug that would dive down around eight feet and hopefully bounce off the wood on the retrieve and *call* a bass out of hiding. Cast one, with the rod tip up, I switched to tip down to get a few more inches of depth as I felt the bait work through the wood and then…it just stopped. Hung up, no, hung on…a BIG bass! I leaned hard on the hooked giant and moved to the center of the boat to position myself to land this massive largemouth bass. Seeing though the relatively clear water I could tell the hook was solidly imbedded in the jaw of the fish, so I decided to play to the camera and make it an extended battle. In what seemed like an eternity but was probably more like 30 seconds, I slid my thumb into the lower lip of a 23½ inch chubby bass that weighed 8½ pounds on a certified scale.

More recently we made a move from a home right on the Rocky River to a new home constructed on the banks of Wood Reservoir around 60 miles away. Now I was completely out of my comfort zone. I had plenty of lake experience but spent more time as a *river rat* in mostly moving waters. After settling in and studying old lake topographical maps, we found and checked several launch points. When traveling to most of the them, we carried a few rods to try our luck off the banks, around a few docks and launch ramp spots. As spring approached, we put our kayaks in and worked a few small coves and backwater pockets with limited success.

As the water heated up so did the fishing. Many of the initial bass we fooled were in the two to three-pound category, but we had heard from the locals this lake had a reputation for producing some truly big bass. Concentrating on a general vicinity located on the northwest side of the lake we began to become familiar with all the visual nuances of this area. Shoreline depths, creek channels, downed wood, middle lake stump fields, and aquatic vegetation. On a summer day when fish seemed to have abandoned the banks, I recalled a solitary deeper water stump we found accidently. I made way over and tied on a chatterbait—not a lure I used often but sometimes you just get a sixth sense feeling. The

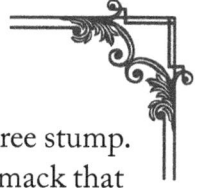

first cast, zero. Second cast felt like it brushed the lone tree stump. Cast number three was a direct hit followed by a solid smack that drove my rod tip toward the water's surface. A heavy, steady pull and then a big splash from a bass that cleared the water by two feet, a BIG, BIG bass. Working this huge fish carefully to the side of my boat I netted a legitimate nine-pounder, all because I applied my intuitive thoughts with a healthy dose of experience and trusting my instincts.

The lessons learned by each of these examples, is don't be intimidated by new spots, believe in your judgement, fish to your strengths, and go where the feeling takes you.

TROPHY TIP: Over the years, whether it was real or imagined I had certain baits that seemed to more often produce trophy fish. I've learned that baits go out of style, colors change annually, companies go out of business and some lures are no longer available. When I find baits that consistently generate BIG bass, I get several. One wooden crankbait from years back, a Poe's #200 in pattern called *spook* was flat out a big fish bait, especially in the fall and when shad are schooled up. I got a dozen and still have several, and they still catch fish. An old Bass Pro Shops bait named by the developer a *Tornado* was a unique combination of a spinnerbait/buzzbait, and it has produced under certain conditions when nothing else would. In stained, cold water I've caught several trophy size bass including a 9½-pound largemouth on this bait. Smallmouth like it too. The fact that two species of bass and others will strike the same bait makes it what I call a *crossover* bait, working on multiple species AND fooling BIG bass. I still have a half dozen in the packaging and four loose in heavily guarded tackle boxes. Old Storm Wiggle Warts, a few Bumble Bee heavy wire spinnerbaits that produced a ten-pound bass and #300 C.A.C. Shiners which fooled a legendary string of small lake bass are all part of my *back-up* big bass baits.

17

Trying New Techniques

At this point in my life I'm admittedly not as good at this experimenting in any form as I should be. I know what works, what I like, and generally what I'm going to use. Experience has taught me, even if it's just a hunch, to pick up certain baits in familiar situations and follow that hunch. I've spent years trying to learn more and mostly attempting to refine my fishing skills. A few years ago, I recognized my limited skills at crankbait fishing, for two seasons I worked at using cranking lures even when I didn't want to. I did get better, caught a few fish, and recognized situations that might produce with one of the various cranking lures. A few big cool water bass on lipless crankbaits earned them a place in a corner of one of my boxes.

With the best of intentions, I packed a few deep water baits in a seasonal box but rarely did they get wet. The squarebill baits became regulars, and now if I see a rock point, a drop-off, or a fallen tree at a 45-degree angle on fast tapering bank my immediate thought is, *Cast that crankbait to those targets.* I own a few jigging spoons but only once tied one on at the urging of a guest while were filming a TV show. We both vertically bobbed these stupid things up and down for a couple of hours, and I finally directed the camera man toward a heavily wooded shoreline. We made the move and began to catch enough jig bass to salvage the show.

My point is, no matter what, it's important to fish in a way

that you enjoy. If you're fishing and not having fun, *you're doing it wrong!*

Why do certain lures and techniques become etched into our fishing brains? *We caught our first fish using* _____ fill in the blank. *We caught a bunch of fish with the* _____. Or my personal favorite, *I caught my BIGGEST fish with this bait.* All reasons for allegiance to a type, size, or color of an artificial bait. I dare say (and I'm guilty of this myself) in the case of certain lures I have three, four, or a dozen of that exact lure! All based off a previous successful experience with it.

Many years ago, a friend and I planned a trip to a small lake. In the excitement and some miscommunication, we both thought we had grabbed my two-sided tackle box, which we later realized was sitting on the back steps of my house. Upon realizing the error, I asked my partner for the day, "Do you have any pork frogs that I can use as a trailer on my jig?"

He responded, "Yes."

"Then I'm fine."

I had a spinnerbait, a jig, and a minnow plug tied on the three rods I brought. I was confident that I was at the least functional with the lures I had. I knew I could cover all three water columns, and this trio of lures had worked well in the past. I caught 41 bass on that memorable day!

A few of the techniques I forced my self to try were the Carolina rig where a heavy weight above a swivel and leader is used to drag a soft plastic bait, often a lizard, around until you feel a bite and the set the worm-style hook. A drop shot, popular in desert lakes around Arizona and California, is normally set up with a bell-style sinker on the end of the line which places it on the bottom, then a smaller hook is attached anywhere from 8 to 12 inches up the line and some plastic bait affixed. Awkward to cast, it's pulled in short strokes and twitched causing the soft plastic to jump and then rest. Not recommended for places with heavy cover because of the exposed hook, I've done it and caught fish on it but...ZZZZZ.

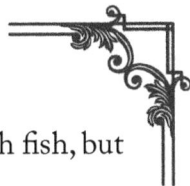

For me it's a snoozer. Both of these techniques will catch fish, but neither is known for fooling truly big bass.

I've migrated to the goal of targeting BIG bass, and I'd rather not be catching anything than catching small fish. This positions me to fish the baits I like in places I choose and not worry about getting skunked or watching the clock. Tournament anglers try to catch five fish—my goal is always to try to catch a FIVE-POUND fish. Interviewing competitive anglers, one comment that I heard often was that they didn't try to necessarily catch big fish and that often it was more accidental then intentional.

I determine my approach by quickly assimilating all the visual information I can and then planning my attack. Because of my preferences, this often leads to my tried and true presentations. Regardless of the type of water craft I've been in, I adopted a stealthy system of moving into an area, utilizing two techniques, pitching and flipping. Often incorrectly described, flipping is a short-range presentation, and pitching is a technique used from a distance generally, at least for me, from 30 feet or so. I pitch to a target area, and if there's no action I might move into the heavy cover and continue trying to get a bite, but the bait offering from a distance is less likely to spook a bass. The underhand pendulum motion is meant to glide just above the surface and barely dimple the water upon entry. If I encounter a spot that looks promising, I look for a presentation point, an opening in the middle of wood or weeds, and then judge the distance to make my pitch. If the cover is dense, I will go closer and flip the spot dropping the bait into cover and watching the line. Often if you've been quiet enough the bait never makes it past the first few feet—a bass will hit the lure based off its natural action.

This brings up a good point, let the bait do what it was designed for, don't overwork it. If the bait touches bottom the line will *curl* and then a *yo-yo* up and down action follows. If you're convinced there's no fish, continue to the next spot. This activity does present the recognition of a pattern very well. Edges, specific depths within

97

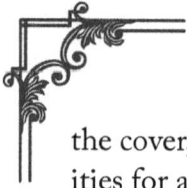

the cover, additional objects like wood or big rock are all possibilities for a strong very repeatable pattern. This is especially true in extreme conditions. Bass will seek overhead cover in clear water, bright skies, cold fronts, or when there's an increased presence of baitfish. I'm willing to pitch any single hook bait for the sake of accuracy and that super silent entry.

Make sure your using the stoutest equipment you have for these techniques. Trying to winch a truly big bass from heavy cover is not a finesse fight, a short string hooked bass is as close to fish combat as you can get. Once sensing the pick-up, you need to swing fast and hard especially of you are trying to move a fish away from heavy cover! As stated previously that bigger bass has probably been hooked before and most likely will try to move into the densest cover close by. This is where the heavy action rod (if you own one) shines. I don't boat flip bass, it will eventually cost you a rod, they become weak and will snap. Having a net handy or moving the fish close to your hand for the grip is vital, many giant fish are lost at this point. Heavy line, sometimes as much as 40-pound braid, with the drag set tight to yield only slightly to the run of a big, big fish and the ability to muscle your trophy out are all important. Don't start thinking about the check you're going to cash or the picture of your prize prematurely.

The Texas rig is likely the most familiar with the bass angler. A slip sinker threaded onto the line, and in my case a red bead is next, and then the worm-style hook of your choice. I use the red bead to protect my knot from the slip sinker, add the red color and produce a clicking sound as the bead knocks between the lead sinker and the top of the hook. For decades the Texas-style rig has been used by bass fisherman all over the world, but there are other ways to rig a plastic bait. One that I'm fond of is the Wacky rig, so named because of an accidental set up by an angler who didn't know how to rig a plastic worm. The story goes upon returning to marina and showing off their catch a couple was asked what they were doing to fool their impressive string of fish. Once they

displayed their "wacky" (where the name came from) rig, it became popular and can be deadly when bass are lazy, highly pressured or just lure shy. Weightless and seemingly hanging in the water column for an extended period of time a wacky rigged soft plastic looks nonthreatening and an easy meal. I have had some success wacky rigging other soft plastic, including bass tubes, lizards, and creature type baits.

The Shakey Head is a relatively simple set up. I merely use a ⅛th ounce sicklehead leadhead, secure a small plastic worm threaded part way up the shank of the leadhead. Make sure you have a straight hang of the worm to keep the line from twisting. The straight hang is equally important because normally this is a worm rig used on spinning tackle—if the worm rotates you will get a line twist that will eventually emerge as *jump-off* of your line and create a mess. Shakey head baits can include smaller crawfish imitators, creature baits, or any other of the popular shapes, sizes, and colors. When the fish are stubborn this will often produce—but don't count on it for a BIG bass bite.

TROPHY TIP: Along with random action, an even bigger factor in boating BIG bass is retrieve speed. This is a tough one to quantify; it's dependent on several factors and sometimes just a gut feel. Suffice to say, making your bait look and move like a genuine food source is a good starting point. Study, any time you can, the natural movements of any living creature in or around the water. Minnows, snakes, frogs, shad, crawfish, bluegill, even dragonflies. All these at one time or another will become a meal for the fish. Match the darting motion of the minnow, the swimming motion of the snake, the hop of the frog (in and out of water) the backwards escape of the crawfish and more. That being said, commit to memory; smaller baits and slower retrieves will almost always catch a few fish. For the biggest fish the important part is the slower retrieve. Retrieve speed, one of the most important concepts to understand AND apply!

18

Lake OR River

While it seems like an easy decision, many times there are angling opportunities that present themselves with no options to choose. In some instances, tournament competitors are given a date and location, and that may place them either on a lake or on a river system. For people that think it doesn't make a difference, read on.

Flat water, aka lakes, are excellent places to try your luck almost any time of the year for multiple species and walking, wading, or boating. With lots of amenities, lakes can offer many desirable attributes, with top notch launch ramps, marinas, concessions, and family friendly atmospheres. Lakes all over draw millions of fishing folks. Depending on the geographic location, lakes hold great populations of bass, bluegill, crappie, catfish, and some are home to lesser known species like walleye, musky, various trout, and more. Lake levels are generally stable with the exception of *pulling* the waters down to winter pool, but because they're landlocked you know the fish aren't going anywhere. Managed by state and government agencies to monitor fish populations, water quality, and safety of the users, lakes receive a lot of attention and financial support. Much of the funding for state agency activities comes from fishermen, duck hunters, and other sources. Manmade structures are a bonus and come in many forms—fishing piers, bridges, rip rap rock banks, and docks can all at times hold fish. Lakes features will create locations for those wanting to try their luck in tournament

competition or maybe locals or even vacationers wanting to stock their freezer with freshly caught fish.

There are many different considerations in choosing between the two water types.

LAKE: Lots of room to roam.

RIVER: Often smaller but longer bodies of water

LAKE: Miles of shoreline.

RIVER: Generally, less shoreline but more distinct cover.

LAKE: A larger area to search.

RIVER: Less of a search based off specific size.

LAKE: Bottom contours, humps, ledges and feeder creeks.

RIVER: Cut banks, inflowing creeks, bends.

LAKE: Select forage food base.

RIVER: Wide variety of food forage.

LAKE: Many times, minimal current.

RIVER: Almost constant current, can position fish predictably.

LAKE: Open water wind effect.

RIVER: Can escape wind more easily.

LAKE: Water levels stable.

RIVER: Unstable water levels due to excessive rain, lack of rain.

LAKE: Can become stagnant during hot weather.

RIVER: Can change its water three times a day.

LAKE: Low oxygen levels.

RIVER: Moving water and vegetation help to maintain oxygen levels.

LAKE: Access to deep water.

RIVER: Not as much deep water to have to search or run.

There's multiple reasons why certain people prefer lakes over rivers or vice versa. In making a case for rivers, I have caught lots of absolute giants from river systems. On most lakes as late winter is giving way to spring, I have had a great deal of success in moving up into the rivers when water temperatures are in the high 40s and the high 50-degree ranges. Then as fall approaches, I follow the schools of bait into the creeks and rivers again. These strategic

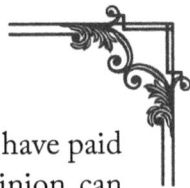

moves are based off bass behavior and experiences that have paid off in trophy catches. The headwaters of lakes, in my opinion, can best be characterized as rivers. The distinction is based more off locations of dams and the opened-up areas seem more a lake environment. The comparisons are endless, and each person can make a case for their favorite. I like the ever-changing shoreline of rivers, the newly added trees falling in, constant shoreline changes, the current, available vegetation, the abundant food sources in a smaller area, less boat traffic, the BIG bass genetics I've found, the muscular build of river bass, and the diversity in almost every ecological area of river systems.

Each lake has a unique personality whether manmade or natural. Dams and the original river channels give an indication as to where to best cast and catch, but each body of water has similarities and unique differences. A major factor for favoring a river system is the presence of current. Learning to read the current and the effects on the fish and its preferred locations is a major plus. Current will position fish to face the moving water for efficiency (less drag and best use of their physical attributes), comfort in the form of cooler water, and a built-in food delivery system. Less effort expended means fish grow bigger and faster. Any object that redirects water is a potential holding area for true trophy bass.

I do believe that a person can become a versatile angler if they spend a lot of time learning and testing their skills in a river environment, the variables mastered in a river prepare the lake fisherman for a wide variety of conditions. I believe a good lake fisherman could easily be perplexed by rivers, while a river fisherman could adjust a little faster to lakes. Big fish are in both, patterns in lakes are probably more solid and day to day more repeatable, and more often pay off than in rivers. The possibility of finding fish faster and setting the hook on a giant is another plus.

Admittedly I'm biased because of my history on rivers. I've caught some absolute monsters in rivers and the headwaters of lakes. Years ago, I made a statement that's often repeated (and

stolen, it's called plagiarism) "There's magic in moving waters." There's just something that draws me to streams, creeks, and rivers.

I can't emphasize enough the element of playing for the current in a river environment. On a trip into the Elk River the headwaters of my home lake, Woods Reservoir, it had become obvious that the recent rain had created a string current flow in the main river. I had faced this several times in the past and discovered a consistent pattern for BIG bass. A small cut, cove, or backwater is used by big fish to minimize the expending of energy to fight the string flow of the river. Just off the current I will venture into the places just off the main river. I look for heavy cover, ambush or resting spots, and the availability of a food source. My second pitch on this day produced a solid seven-pound bass, and later I pulled four more good fish from the school that had formed there. This pattern has paid off so many times it's a go-to tactic for me. I rely of three specific lure choices; the jig, a Texas rigged soft plastic, or a modified spinnerbait. The jig with the fixed head gives me good lure control in feeling the bait coming through, the Texas rig gives me the option of multiple sizes and colors, and the spinnerbait gives a momentary flash that shines in the heavily stained waters. I replace the back blade of the spinnerbait with a hammered copper-colored blade for a different look ,and this river special has been deadly for trophy sized bass. My biggest was a nine and a half-pound largemouth resting along a thick weed bed.

Other potential fast flowing river presentations are a squarebill crankbait around wood or a big bladed dark skirted buzzbait. It's worth mention that Debbie's biggest bass to date, a fat eight-pound largemouth, came on (what else) her beloved Ragetail soft plastics. Her biggest smallmouth, a six plus-pounder, came from the Caney Fork River.

TROPHY TIP: A hidden flaw that many people (including myself) make is what I refer to as a *negative forward flow*. Over-looked or hidden in many misses on a big bass were faulty hook

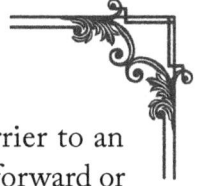

sets due to a well disguised error in recognizing a barrier to an efficient hook set. Whether your water craft is drifting forward or the trolling motor or even the wind has you traveling toward your bait there's an automatic slack line effect. Consequently, as you try to make up line or take up slack you could possibly get weak connection between the rod and the fish. This flaw could cause a barely hooked bass, a complete miss, or the loss of your fish during the battle to the boat. Taking up the appropriate amount of line before a set is crucial to how deeply and securely a bass is hooked. For this reason, I try to fish aware of the forward flow, cast and present the bait toward the banks or even with the water craft, or even opposite of the flow meaning the back of the boat. Think of this as the opposite of trolling which gives you a solid set because of the forward motion and the naturally tight line. Not a fan of anchoring, but it does give you a static position (no movement) to cast, retrieve, and set the hook.

19

Those Other Bass

While there are millions of anglers who proclaim they are bass fishermen, they use the term generically for the major player of the bass family, the largemouth bass. There are though those who are loyal to the other two less famous members in the bass family, the spotted aka Kentucky bass and the hard fighting smallmouth bass. I must admit while I've caught thousands of each, I'm still far from the expert on what I consider the less available bass.

Seeing Spots—One observation for me is that if I'm in search of largemouth, and I catch two spotted bass, I move. It's my contention they'll drive the largemouth crazy. Spots will take over and area and feed on the same forage as the more popular bass. They also come off as more aggressive in behavior. I do know that like many other anglers, if I'm going to keep fish, I will clean my catch of spotted bass without hesitation. They generally have good numbers and, because they are in competition with the other two bass, eat lots and lots of crawfish, the main and preferred food source of the both the large and smallmouth bass. It makes sense with less Kentucky's there are more crawfish. If fishing for spots anything that mimics or matches crawfish is a great choice. Try smaller jigs, trailed by soft plastic craws and especially in natural or local craw colors. Smaller spinners and minnow plugs will catch their share of Kentucky bass. Another option is the shakey head

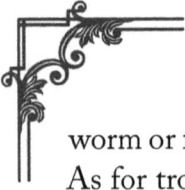

worm or finesse-type worms rigged on a small ⅛th ounce leadhead. As for trophy size fish, because they normally are abundant, they will normally exist in big numbers and decrease their own natural food supplies. True trophy fisheries for spots are in the deep south and norther California.

THEORY: Populations of spotted bass are also increased because of their spawning habits. Go earlier, invade, and take over areas and finite food supply

The Mysterious Smallmouth Bass, the Original Frequent Fliers—
Often tough to pattern and even more difficult at times to get to bite, smallmouth are loved by many and hated by others for their ability to disappear quickly. Another aspect of the smallmouth that confounds anglers is their love of deep water. Different than their cousins the largemouth bass, you can catch them in shallow waters at times and in rivers that have less deep water or even just a few isolated holes, but the lake inhabitants love deep, cool, clear environments. Tough, tenacious fighters and vicious lure strikers the smallmouth does things that go against the grain of those who try to force largemouth tactics on the *brown* bass.

Having said that, there are enough similarities to confuse the most seasoned veteran bass anglers. A spinnerbait rolled down the side of a point, and *boom*, a smallmouth crushes it. Or maybe a crankbait run across a deeper point, perfect place for a largemouth, and a smallmouth hammers the bait. A stump field in a cove has that largemouth look and a buzzbait weaving though the wood, and *bang*, a huge hit from a smallmouth bass. They all seem to contradict the deep-water theory, but these incidents are more the exception than the rule.

Tales of the old-time experts almost always came with the advice to fish a "hair fly and pork rind" or a grub threaded on a leadhead and jut swim it back to the boat. Because they prefer deep water, they can be schooled up and produce some legendary catches.

Rarely do I target smallmouth, but if I were looking to tangle with a few, I'd have a mix of baits AND wouldn't rule out live bait!

After years of guiding summer wilderness trips in Canada, I learned much more about this species. They do prefer water that seems to range from eight feet to 25 feet. Depth preference varies according to what's available. River fish will seek mid-stream positions below riffles, parallel to big submerged logs, points, bluff type banks, and even vegetation growing out towards the middle. Learning to read moving waters regardless of the target species is critical. Watching for inside bends or outside bends is a clue as to favored hideouts, resting places, and ambush points. The inside bends receive a heavier flow and make objects that defect the current desirable. The outside bends get much of the force from rushing water and position fish on the back side of the bend where water will eventually slow. The river smallmouths are *muscled up*, hit, and fight hard.

The baits in my tackle box that give me the best chance to tangle with *smallies* intentionally include jigs in two sizes. Because they like cold water, which is generally clearer, I like the downsize version trailed by the smaller craw imitation. If you're a fan of the spinnerbait, I have tremendous success with an altered bait, a chartreuse back blade with a dash of red on it, and if you're an after-hours angler and like the night bite, a spinner is highly effective. Beware, the slamming stop of the spinnerbait smallmouth bite is the second most addictive hit from these fish. While they will hit hard plugs, crankbaits, jerkbaits, and the lipless models, the topwater bite is the one that will test your nerves and heart. Dog walkers, propeller baits, cup face poppers, and easily my favorite— the buzzbait, any of these can potentially produce a surface hit that will splash you all the way back into the boat.

Lou Williams, a legend on Pickwick lake and others, has boated thousands of smallmouth bass and suggests that crankbaits and spinnerbaits will catch more fish, but for trophy size smallies he's trying 3 or 4 inch grubs or a creature bait fishing drop-offs near deep water.

A deadly system, if you have the time and place to try it, is the slow drift of live bait. While this tactic will produce several species, I have tremendous results on winter smallmouth or stubborn largemouth using a specific system. Looking for a trophy, read on.

I learned this technique fishing with The Bass Professor Doug Hannon. We caught golden shiners to use as bait for Florida largemouth. He had heavy action rods, baitcasting reels spooled with 40 pound test line, and hooks he had surgically sharpened. Retrieving a hand-sized shiner from the bait well we would lip hook the bait and lay beside the boat so as not to harm the shiner by casting, then let out around 30 feet of line and begin a slow drift hold line just below the fourth rod guide and between our fingers with the reel in free spool. You can feel the golden shiner swimming along and when a fish began to follow the bait would signal through the line a nervous attempt to flee. The hit was a solid thump at which point you release the line and count to seven, engage the reel and set the hook…hard! The only difference for me was I would seine the biggest creek minnows I could find and be drifting out of a flat bottom boat in a river system. You could watch the smallmouth *track* the big minnow, follow, and hit the bait. Occasionally I ran a natural cork float to be able to see the float disappear. Deadly in clear water, this produced some of the best numbers and biggest smallmouth of my life, one a legitimate six-pounder. You don't have to forget everything you know about largemouth just know the ways of the brown bass. In short, don't try to force largemouth tactics on a smallmouth.

TROPHY TIP: If you have access to or own (I've had both) your own body of water, a tip that will increase your chances of a trophy fishery is related to how you manage and what you stock in your personal lake. Stock NO crappie in smaller bodies of water (less than 25 acres). They have a tendency to over-populate if not harvested. Crappie will spawn before bass, meaning the bass will eat less of the fry. Additionally the bass will spawn, and the post spawn

crappie will feed on the bass fry. Also, bass, because of the spiny rays/fins of the crappie, avoid eating them when they get larger. Likewise, green sunfish will over-populate a body of water quickly with multiple spawns per year and compete with the bass for forage. If you add additional food by seining, minnows, or other sources you risk the spread of invasive aquatic vegetation and disease from accidental transfer of other creatures, plants, or organisms.

20

Small Waters—BIG bass

A check of many of the bass state records would show smaller waters have more than their share of notable catches. At least 20 of the 49 state records (there are no largemouth bass in Alaska) show that largemouth records come from ponds, smaller private lakes, and other undersized waters.

Why do small waters produce BIG bass?
- Less fishing pressure and fish get a chance to grow.
- Fertile waters often fed by small creeks providing additional oxygen AND food sources.
- Small waters can be better managed by harvest and intentional supplemental feeding.
- Management for trophy fishing by removal of small fish.
- Stocking of certain strains capable of quick growth and large sizes.
- Minimal fishing/boating pressure.
- Better genetics from brood type fish.

I've had the privilege of fishing smaller private lakes and for years even my own pond. Most of the places were carefully managed with the goal of producing mega bass. The opportunity to fish places where you know fish in the six to ten pound category swim is exciting. In my own case, my pond was a test laboratory stocked with the ultimate goal of a trophy fishery. Starting from scratch the pond was dug to my specifications. I left an island for access and additional shoreline, banks were sloped properly to minimize the growth of unwanted vegetation, big boulder rocks were intentionally stacked in deeper water. The maximum depth was 11 feet, and the pond was fed by the sloping landscape surrounding the area. Gravel was added in a few spots to facilitate spawning. A couple of willow trees were left on the banks to draw bugs and create shade. Before the pond filled, I cut some good size dead cedar tree branches, took five-gallon buckets, turn the trees upside down (the downward facing branches were less likely to snag baits) and added concrete to create long lasting tree and brush for cover, and distributed the buckets strategically throughout the pond bottom. I introduced bluegill, a few months later fingerling bass, and later in the year I took a risk and seined bait, mostly minnows and crawfish, from the cleanest, healthiest stream I could find, hoping I wasn't bringing any disease in. During the second year I slowly added bigger fish I was catching and relocating with the intent to have brood fish. It worked! Almost anytime I fished I could be assured of catching a trophy size bass. The bluegill fishing was also excellent.

Also notable are places where there are forgotten lakes and ponds. Dug, formed, or natural these spots have the potential for big catches. One place has three little lakes, creek fed and fertilized naturally but not fished often. Typical catches are more of the *cookie cutter* type bass running between 10 and 12 inches, but occasionally one lake gives up a true trophy bass. The difference is a creek flowing through, some heavy stump spots, thick aquatic vegetation emergence in the late spring and through the summer months, and fairly abundant food sources. Essentially this one place has all the critical criteria to producing BIG bass. This all lends credence to the *four factors* previously mentioned—oxygen, food, cover, and a deep-water escape.

Many of my best catches also occurred on close to home public waters. I had several river systems that received minimal pressure and had no stocked fish but seemingly excellent genetics.

Others were headwaters for a major lakes, rivers that for years went unspoiled. On the plus side, there was minimal development, not much erosion damage, no hazardous spills, little fishing pressure, a healthy flow, feeder creeks, abundant and diverse food supply, and other species of superior size indicating ideal conditions. Dozens of BIG bass came from various stretches of a particular river. A four-pound spotted Kentucky bass, several smallmouths over five pounds, and largemouth, oh the largemouth! Fish in the five to seven-pound category were common and occasionally the magical, almost mythical dream ten-pound bass was landed, and one day in the late spring I lipped an eleven-pound three-ounce absolute giant. All my big bass are released with the exception of one that I couldn't resuscitate. It hangs on my wall as reminder of a great catch but also to keep in mind the careful handling of any bass especially those that make it to the superior size.

Handling and Successful Release—BIG bass are such a precious resource it's critical to make sure we do all we can so they survive and thrive. I love watching them swim back home! It all starts with the hooking of the fish. I try with the jig or worm fish to set the hook as soon as I realize I'm getting bit. If you don't react quickly, often fish will swallow the bait and be deeply hooked. A bleeding fish is likely to die, but I would still release it giving it chance. If the fish has swallowed the bait completely some suggest clipping the line which does work sometimes. If I can feel the lure down in the thorax (the throat closure) of the fish I push my first two fingers together to try and minimize hook damage and keep pressure on the hook guarding the barb, pulling gently to dislodge the bait, and hopefully recovering the bait without damage to the fish.

When possible, I try to lip land my fish regardless of size. I do carry a landing net; it's rubberized netting helps reduce damage to the fish's fins and body slime. When handling a bass, it's vital to the fish to not touch the eyes or the gills, either can signal eventual bacterial infection and ultimately death to the bass. There is such

115

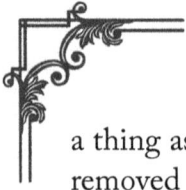

a thing as delayed mortality for fish that have had the slime coat removed by poor handling. This can create something similar to a burn bacterial infection which dooms the fish.

Also because of the difference in air pressure and water pressure it's important to support the weight of the fish (with wet hands) so as to not damage the internal organs. Another consideration is to not throw the fish high in the air on the release—it's like a belly flop for the bass and can cause internal damage. A quick picture and immediate release is the best bet.

Sizzling summer temperatures pose a completely different dilemma! There is a diminished amount of dissolved oxygen when surface water temperatures rise into the eighties. Bass and other species have difficulties breathing and when they are strained from a long battle at the end of your line can experience a build up of lactic acid from the fight and have something similar to a total body *Charlie horse* and sink to the bottom then die. With warmer water extremes, get the bass in as quickly as possible and try to release them immediately. Big bass are way to valuable to be caught just once. Good practices can allow them to live to fight (and spawn) another season.

State managed lakes have also proven to be good locations for trophy bass. Most state agencies manage more for quantity than quality, but there are exceptions. The general public are more satisfied with just catching fish and not necessarily aiming for trophies. The government agencies set goals for a good population and a renewable resource. It's difficult to manage public waters for numbers *and* size. The science involved is a constantly changing scenario. State waters can and do produce trophy fish, but their task isn't limited to bass and certainly not bigger fish. Bigger fish are a biproduct of good genetics, adequate food sources, clean water, and some luck. Funding doesn't allow for intensive work, but the shocking studies, creel surveys, hatchery work as well as stocking Florida strains are all a gigantic help in the hopes of trophy bass fishing.

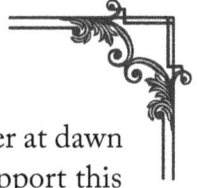

TROPHY TIP: There's an old adage that bass bite better at dawn and dusk. While there was no scientific evidence to support this then back in the day, there is now. The eyes of the bass adjust to lower light levels faster than the eyes of shad and other baitfish. This physical phenomenon gives the bass family a decided advantage over the food source they feed on the most frequently. Taking advantage of these times can increase your chances of baiting a "Big Un."

21

Adjustments

When you get the feeling that something isn't working (other than just not getting a bite), follow that feeling. Consider making an adjustment. For me that negative feeling could be the wrong type of cover in an area, a wind shift, cloud cover moving in (or out), seeing a different water color, no forage base in the area, or just the sense that you should make a change in baits or boat positioning or move to another spot.

I was fishing in a pretournament practice with one of the all-time legendary anglers on the Colorado river. We moved to a spot that had a shoreline covered in what are called bulrushes or cattails. Faced with gin clear warm water we started throwing topwater baits and would watch as several fish came up, briefly stared at the surface lures, stalled, and slowly turned away disappearing into deeper water. I suggested the bass were actually seeing us and maybe a move to parallel that same bank with the hope that might produce different results. It worked! Now the same bass began to hit the original baits we were casting but now had a shorter window on vision. We simply made a small adjustment.

A lesson from the trout fishing community is to let the bait *drift*. Normal current or wind movement in no way spooks the fish. Most of us are too impatient to present a lure this way, but to a bass it looks natural and normal in their underwater world. Many people make the error of overworking a bait.

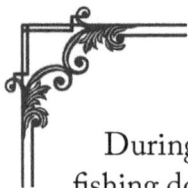

During the winter it's often been my experience that the bass fishing doesn't pick up until the afternoon, we commonly call this the *afternoon bite*. A full sun in the right spot warms the water a few degrees and has proven to be enough to trigger the fish to become active. Any kind of hard surface, gravel, sand, concrete bridge pilings, or boulder rock all are likely location for the afternoon bite. It may be a short window of opportunity, a fifteen or twenty-minute feeding span, but possibly the best chance to pick up a good fish. An adjustment I've seen payoff especially in the late spring and summer is to seek out the heaviest cover in the most remote area of the lake. A remote area may be just off the boat trails, in the back of coves or up into headwaters.

THEORY: Normal boating and fishing pressure can drive bass deeper into places farther than their normal haunts and secondarily push them into submerged wood, thick weeds, way back into lily pads or under abandon docks.

If you're trolling, drifting, or being pushed by the current it can create a hook-setting dilemma. I've described this as a negative forward flow. The forward motion as you make a retrieve can easily throw a slack in your line making it difficult to get a solid set. Try changing your casting direction to create *drag* on your bait and remove the looping slack line.

A shad spawn, bluegill spawn, a hatch of frogs, mayflies, or the presence of dragonflies may also be a clue to a switch in tactics. During the shad spawn (generally late summer) I keep a small topwater lure available to throw into the bass busting the giant schools of shad. Gizzard or threadfin shad spawn at water temperatures of around 68–75 degrees. The bluegill will spawn at 70 degrees and on the full moon. When you locate nesting bluegill, bass won't be too far away. Bass of all types love to dart in and raid the nest of the fry (baby bluegill) but even more so do the adults. A few years ago, I saw a honeycomb indicating a large set of

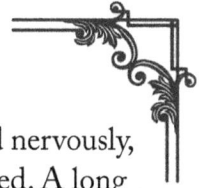

spawning bluegill beds. The bluegills were circling around nervously, and I immediately grabbed a rod with a buzzbait attached. A long arching cast past the beds drew a strike from an eight-pound river largemouth. The shoreline appearance of leopard and bullfrogs are also a signal to heave those imitation frogs. The appearance of Mayflies and dragonflies are a tipoff to an underutilized pattern, as the bugs hatch they will use aquatic vegetation to stop on and wait, the bluegill recognize the large presence of bugs and will stage around the same cover which simultaneously draw bass in to become part of the chain of feeding cycle. Casting to a similar area, same scenario, a *rice crispies* sound drew my attention to the vegetation disturbance. Bluegill were laying in wait as dragonflies landed and took off the lily pads, and bass, hearing the sound of fish feeding, invaded the spot. A slow drift right into the middle of a *field* of dollar pads produced several bass, and in the very back along a creek channel, I landed a nine-pound largemouth!

In order to make presentation adjustments, I carry what I refer to as situational baits. A few examples might be, when I find *dirty*, muddy, heavily stained water I make sure I have a few bigger baits, some with rattle chambers, a couple of different contrasting colors of jigs, and specialized spinnerbaits. I take my normal ⅜th ounce spinner and alter the bait by attaching a single oversized (#7 ½) copper colored willowleaf blade. In each instance I'm appealing to the most used sense of the bass, the sense of sight. In clear water try smaller baits. I've caught good size bass on small crappie type soft plastics attached to a ⅛th ounce leadhead. Finesse jigs, four or five inch plastic worms, and undersized crankbaits or spinners are all possible options for extremely clear waters.

My tackle boxes also have the proven winners residing in the trays that have earned a spot in the my boxes.

THEORY: In competing with thousands of the same size shad or other normal forage, your bait has to stand out. A BIG bass tactic is offering a bigger meal for the fish who is expending the

same amount of energy to chase down the meal, given the choice the bigger meal (if properly presented) is more likely to get hit by a trophy. Bigger is most often better but if improperly presented offers distinct clues to being artificial and will be rejected.

Dirty water or darkness disguises flaws in line diameter, presentation or lure size. Consider appealing to the hearing of the bass sound or go silent. When choosing baits also know that the eyes of the bass collect light five times better than their apex predator, man. Studies show bass can see up to 30 feet in clear water, and red shows up better than any other color. On cloudy days, in stained water and windy conditions, light penetration is reduced, and fish will move more freely and even go shallow. With less visibility hearing and use of lateral line comes into play, and be advised; the misconception of the degree of the sense of smell in bass rarely draw strikes.

Weather related adjustments would include going to the wind-blown shore and tossing a spinnerbait to opportunistic bass feeding on the baitfish and crawfish drawn to the churning waters and the small microscopic meals produced by the disturbed waters. Rain pushing waters in from secondary creeks and runoff delivers extra oxygen, cooler water, and some potential food source readily available to the bass staged and waiting near the immediate affected areas.

One of my favorite adjustments is the altering of lures. Just a few lure changes are putting a larger/heavier hook on front of crankbait to pull the nose down and make it less likely to get hung up. I replace front crankbait treble hooks with a red treble giving the bait a subtle red flash while in motion. Another effective alteration is the conversion of a double willowleaf bladed spinner to a single blade. I clip the front blade off and add a shad pattern skirt for a fabulous fall season shad imitation. With my soft plastics, be they a plastic worm, craw, or otherwise making a color change through the use of an orange or red Spike-It marker has proven

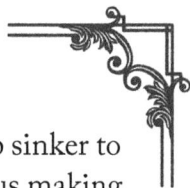

effective for lure shy bass. I have also scrapped a lead slip sinker to expose the shiny lead under the oxidized dull surface thus making a subtle eye-catching attraction. Each of these might appear to be minimal, but doing something different is a great tactic to fooling lure shy bass.

When you want to cast a heavier jig or spinner you might consider simply adding a *pinch-on* sinker weight making your bait more castable and increasing the fall rate without changing baits. Just pinch the sinker onto the shaft of the hook. I found it handy to also carry replacement skirts for spinners, jigs, and buzzbaits. No need to retie if just the skirt is degraded. Just pull the old damaged skirt off and slid the new one on. You can also slow the fall of any jig by replacing the skirt with a bulkier specialized spinnerbait skirt. I use one from Strike King marketed under the title *perfect skirt*.

Be willing to experiment with making moves and various adjustments to give your bait and the bass different looks.

TROPHY TIP: When fishing a jig or soft plastic bait, continue the twitching motion all the way back. I've caught hundreds of fish on the retrieve by merely keeping the lure twitching and moving until it's all the way back to the boat or bank. I've have caught hundreds of fish just by being aware and doing this. Be prepared: a bass may well *short string* you by hitting the bait with you having about six inches of line out.

22

Myths or Misconceptions

Where The Bass Live—While everyone has an opinion as to the home place of a bass, there are few fool proof descriptions of where bass spend most of their time. The truth is, any area that serves all their needs is likely to hold fish any time of the year. Oxygen, food, cover, and deep water are the requirements. Find these areas, find the fish. These compacted places are gold mines for good fish.

What They Eat—The simple answer here—if it will fit in their mouth, a bass will eat it. Preference, crawfish, then shad, then blue-gill...after that anything imaginable, other game fish, birds, baby ducks, snakes, frogs, baby muskrats, and you name it. BIG bass are opportunistic feeders, if it happens close by, any bass, especially a BIG one, will make a meal of it.

The Spawning Cycles—Spring pre-spawn is a great time to catch bass of all sizes, later during the spawn bass can be "fooled" into picking up a bait to move it off the nest, but they DO NOT feed while spawning. Also, the excuse for not catching fish because they're *all on bed* doesn't fly—they don't *all* do the same thing at the same time. Post-spawn bass move deeper and begin to rest and then feed. The primary criteria for spawning are water temperature followed by moon phase.

Don't Hate On The Bass—One of my favorite misconceptions is that bass are described as hating something and hitting it because they *hate* it. Bass hit to feed or defend their nesting area while guarding fry (little bass). To intimate that bass get mad is attributing human emotions to a fish, and unless you tell me you can make a bass happy, I don't personally believe you can make one mad. While doing seminars at a bait show I heard another speaker claim that bass hated turtles while he was casting a soft plastic turtle into the big observation tank (coincidentally he was selling the same baits). The bass instinctively hit the fake bait, but the fish were hatchery raised, and the flaw in his statement was that these bass had never actually seen a turtle before.

Bass Go Deep In Summer/Winter—*Deep* is a relative term. In a small lake, deep could be eight feet, in a highland reservoir deep could be 40 feet. Bass go where they feel safe and can breathe and eat. Most tournament people would describe themselves as power fishermen—some of the most successful of these focus on shallow water. With the widespread use of Forward Facing Sonar, anglers are loading up on fish that were previously not targeted. Once bass are pushed enough and become condition, watch as their behavior changes.

THEORY: Bass spend most of their time shallow. They go to *thin* water to spawn and eat and most often go to deeper water when threatened, there's a seasonal drawdown, or the food sources move. There are many more feeding opportunities in shallow water.

Best Bait Colors—Your favorite color is going to be the one that worked best for you or the one that produced your biggest bass. There are advantages to subtle colors; they are more likely to fool a big, experienced fish. In color selection consider contrast—brighter is rarely better. The only exception is heavily stained/muddy water. Colors that match the food sources are

good but along with the profile, size and action of the bait each has its place.

THEORY: In waters that receive a lot of fishing pressure, the continuous exposure to the same color bait can condition fish to ignore it. If a bass, especially a big one, has been caught multiple times it will often snub the lure type and color it's already had a negative experience with. This is why random action is so critical to consistently fooling bigger bass.

Equipment Needs vs Wants—Those with the most toys aren't always the best fishermen. We all often fall into the trap of thinking the newest equipment is going to be what helps us catch more and bigger fish. The truth is, becoming really adept with a few lures and techniques probably positions you better to catch a monster bass than having a huge tackle box and four dozen rods.

Always/Never—Quite simply, in dealing with any form of outdoor activity, the use of *always* and n*ever* should be discouraged. Bass or whitetail bucks, crappie or ducks, they will rarely fall into the category of always or never. Rarely do I use either term, always or never.

Take Zero Fish—The controversy rages over people harvesting versus releasing their catch. I would personally never eat any big fish—bass, crappie, catfish...whatever. I will take *cookie cutter* bass occasionally, keep crappie in the fall, and clean a stringer of bluegill for a fish fry. My position remains: if an angler catches a fish of any size that is legal, they're entitled to do what they please with it. What's legal and what's ethical is where there exists a dilemma. Ethically it's a better choice to release a bigger fish to spawn. It helps to understand they are the most efficient predators, keeping a balance in waters of all sizes but especially smaller bodies of water.

Stock Florida Bass Everywhere—While they grow to epic sizes and fight harder, Florida bass aren't meant for all places. They physically don't thrive or even survive under certain circumstances—water temperatures being one of the most important factors. Florida strain bass just don't do well everywhere. Trust the science on this one.

BIG Bass Behavior—On my email is a quote by me I've used for years, "Llittle bass are liars, BIG bass hold all the secrets." Truly BIG bass are a different breed from the *run of the mill* fish. The typical bass eats often, and that's what gets them caught. A BIG bass eats even more often, and that's how they get big *and* stay big. The logical question then is, *Why are they hard to catch?* They develop survival skills that make them the superior of the species. Little bass charge at anything that even slightly resembles a food source; big bass seek a safe spot and inspect things more closely, listen, or look for a flaw in the object. They learn avoidance.

There's One Pattern—You could put Denny Brauer and Keven VanDam on the same lake in different spots, and Brauer would develop a strong jig pattern while Van Dam would put together a solid crankbait pattern. The point; several specific but different patterns can easily be going on the very same lake at the very same time. The key here for the trophy hunter is to not get lulled into going outside of their experience and be satisfied that while others are fishing for quantity, your fishing for quality. There's a difference.

Just Release the Fish, It'll Be Fine—Mishandling a bass dooms it to death even though it may take a few days. There's a difference in air pressure and water pressure. Support the belly of the bass so as to not damage the internal organs. Along the same lines, do not flip a bass into the air like it's an Olympic diver—same reason, same result. If you use a landing net, the rubberized netting isn't as likely to damage the fins or remove the slime coat. Removal of

the slime coat through mishandling or over-handling will lead to a bacterial infection eventually killing the fish. Try to not touch the eyes or the gills and gill rakers (the red part inside the gill covering).

Bass "Think"—In relation to body size, a bass has a small brain. Like any wild creature they react to an external stimulus. A reaction is not *thinking*, it's tapping into previous experience or a positive or negative sensory trigger. Like most creatures, they can be conditioned by repeated exposure, but that doesn't compare to a cognitive thought process. There can be predictable responses from almost any creature, but that doesn't indicate *thinking*—it's just a survival response.

Live Bait is Cheating—Being good at live bait presentation is difficult to master but highly effective; that's why it's outlawed in tournaments. The number one reason live bait is effective is it presents no negative clues. It looks, swims, and behaves like exactly what it is—alive. Salt water and freshwater anglers both tap into this type of presentation. Fishing with shiners is a lesson of its own. Live, wild caught shiners exhibit a fear and flight response when pursued by bass, this merely triggers the bass into the chase or cat and mouse scenario. For commercially raised bait this response doesn't exist, there's not the natural fear, maybe more of a curiosity that gets them in trouble.

I Can Use One Rod for Every Application—Any rod will cast, facilitate the retrieve, and give some sort of hook set, BUT there's a better rod for many of the different techniques. I prefer a medium heavy or heavy action rod with a fast tip for my jig/plastic worm fishing (the rod action is generally found on the base of the rod just above the handle). For crankbaits, spinnerbaits, and topwater, I like a medium action rod, and for lighter lures a medium action spinning outfit. The retrieve speed on the reel should match the technique. Today's rods are lighter, reels faster, but if you're targeting

BIG bass keep in mind the outfit has to have the *guts* to get the job done.

A Fish That's Been Caught Won't Bite Again for Days—Maybe. The external factors might matter more. Years ago, during a Missouri wintertime fishing trip, I had a unique experience. Facing cold water conditions so I chose to use a simple live bait set up. Using spinning equipment, I had a container of nightcrawlers and would thread the crawlers about an inch up on a #1 heavy hook with two small split shot pinched on 6 inches above the hook. I would cast the worm out and simply use a super slow retrieve dragging the worm across the bottom. After sensing a *pick-up* I would pause and the set the hook. I reeled up several pale fish from the 43-degree water, I was tagging bigger bass with an identification tag attached just behind the anterior dorsal fin for a growth survey project on this private lake. While working an area I had visited earlier, I returned to see if there were any left in the area. I got the signal a fish had hit the bait, a sharp set, and I reeled in a surprise—the bass I had tagged earlier, the three-pound bass bit, it was same fish again! The cold water had numbed the fish's reaction to the experience enough that it hit again less that 30 minutes after being hooked and landed.

23

Seasonal Suggestions

Spring; Everyone's Favorite—After the long layoff of winter, spring is welcomed by bass fishermen everywhere. Speaking geographically, winter in Wisconsin is worse than winter in Florida, but weather and water everywhere is generally cooler. In Tennessee we get just enough cold weather to make the seasons distinctly different. Spring does offer the promise of all things wild emerging and ready eat, bloom, and grow.

For bass it's a combination of the warmer weather and water that sends the signal, "It's to feed and prep for the spawn." Both these factors combine to provide the potential for some of the best bass fishing of the year. With everything right, you can just open your tackle box and attach almost any bait to the end of the line and catch a few fish, and this gives many people the false illusion that they have mastered bass fishing. Because most people *run the bank*, it's now that big bass can be caught even if it's accidental.

For me, the jig is a bait without seasonal restrictions, spinnerbaits can be lethal, for bass chasing bait the crankbait is a good choice ,and before long topwater time is upon you. Soft plastic will get you bit, and you can catch bass in great numbers while the water is in the 60 to 70 degree range.

This also the time to suggest an equipment intervention. Used reels need to be lubed, old line changed, dull hooks sharpened, and a restocking of your tackle box are all in order. Fish are scattered,

but bank beaters and those looking for largemouth are rewarded frequently. Shoreline cover, any kind or size of rock, docks, submerged trees, and just about any object is a likely holding spot. Smallmouth bass may have already done their thing. Spring is a great time for bass fishing folks of all degrees of skill.

Big Bass Baits: ⅜th ounce jigs in crawfish colors and trailed by a soft plastic crawfish, crankbaits in shad patterns, ⅜th to ½ ounce buzzbaits, spinnerbaits ⅜th ounce Colorado/willowleaf bladed white skirted spinners, and double Colorado models are all special in the spring. You can add floating worms rigs to the list in the spring and early summer.

Summer; Turn Dog Days into Hog Days—Smallmouth have long ago moved into the deeper spots and abandon the banks. Largemouth are no longer *looking for love* and roam along cover, creek channels, points, and bottom contours that can confound the bass angler.

Where'd they go?

With skyrocketing water temperatures, bass of all three major species are eating, quickly digesting due to high metabolic rates fueled by the warmer water, and then searching for their next meal. Surface water temps of 75–85 are not unusual during typical southern summer months. BIG bass have to eat to maintain or gain weight, but how they go about it now may be different than any other time of the year. Heavy cover of any kind is a holding, resting, and ambush point for heavyweight largemouth. Smallmouth are content to raid deeper bluegill beds, roam the rocky areas for crawfish, and pick off shad from massive bait schools.

This is the time of year I go to summertime tactics such as a surface frog in pads, grass, and mazes of downed trees. I rely on large Texas rigged worms to tempt bass along edges and in deeper tangled spots where they may become lazy but are willing to hit something presented to within inches of their hideout. A silent approach and presentation pay off now. Early morning buzzbaits

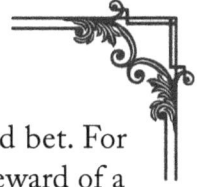

and crankbaits around secondary structures are a good bet. For the adventurous angler willing to brave the dark, the reward of a giant bass may be the prize.

Always popular soft plastics, slow rolling and bottom bumping spinnerbaits are a good after-hours tactic, and the now ignored topwater bite from an old school Arbogast Jitterbug will rekindle memories. Any color at night is good—as long as it's black.

Big Bass Baits: Finesse jigs ¼ ounce with smaller trailers, seven to ten-inch plastic worms Texas rigged, white or black skirted buzzbaits for fishing at dawn and dusk, ½ to ¾ ounce single Colorado blade dark skirted spinnerbaits, deep diving crankbaits, Black topwater plugs, wake baits, dog walkers, cup faced poppers.

Fall; They Have to Eat—A phrase I've used over and over is "everything eats in October." Now it's time for the bass family to prepare for the impending winter months. The drive to feed is automatic, and they will gorge themselves on anything that comes reasonably close to them. Huge shad schools are pursued by bass, the need to feed pushes the fish to follow the schools of shad, their main food supply for weeks now.

The shorter days and falling water temperatures are indicators that winter is coming. Bass are not discriminating now, and there is competition for any forage. Twice I've caught two bass on the same cast using shad colored crankbaits in off-shore environments. It's not uncommon to catch fish that look like they will burst from bellies loaded with crawfish, shad, bluegill, or anything resembling a meal. As water temperatures fall, bass will remain active until around 50 degrees and then start to slow up from a metabolic standpoint. Slowly some food sources disappear or become less available—bugs, crawfish, snakes, and others *bury up* in the cold, but shad and bluegill are still around. Fall is great for numbers or a true trophy.

Big Bass Baits: Shad mimicking lures, single willowleaf blade spinnerbait with a glimmer type skirt, large bladed buzzbaits

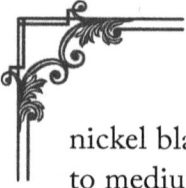

nickel blade white skirt plus shad pattern crankbaits in shallow to medium divers, ⅜th ounce jigs, wacky rigged stick worms are all considerations.

Winter: What To Look For In The Winter—Cold water catches of BIG bass can happen in the winter months. The keys are finding schools of bait fish and water that might be two or three degrees warmer. The Northwest side of the lake is a good place to begin (with the sun rising in the East and setting in the West the Northwest sections get more exposure to the sun). Couple sun with the presence of rock, sand, gravel, or even concrete launch ramps and you have a likely set up for warmer waters. Bass are still in slowdown mode, but a properly presented bait will draw a strike even if it's a lazy bite or a no chase situation. Gone are green weeds but underwater wood is still a popular hangout. Don't dismiss live bait in the dead of winter! Big creek minnows, live shad, even nightcrawler worms can attract attention and a hit. The colder the water, go to smaller lures and slower retrieves. Go with the mindset that you may be fishing for just two or three bites.

Big Bass Baits: A white swim jig with a white soft plastic swimbait attached, a suspending jerkbait (clown color is awesome), a ¼ to ⅜th ounce jig fished with a slow presentation, a flatside crankbait for a wide wobble in shad colors, a short arm spinner bait with a single nickel colored blade and a white skirt mimics a dying shad, old fashioned air jig fished with no trailer in white or brown/orange should be in your winter tackle box.

In Case You Were Wondering—Here are the reasons I don't fish a Carolina, A-Rig or jigging spoon:
- A Carolina rig doesn't travel well through heavy cover and is more of a search bait for me. I've never caught a fish bigger than three pounds using this technique.
- The A-Rig requires specialized equipment. Ask anyone who has thrown it how many rods they broke because of the

pressure and strain it puts on a regular rod. The rig itself is expensive and needs several soft plastic baits to attach to the multiple hooks and teaser arms.

- The jigging spoon to me is one of the most boring ways to fish that there is in existence. Dropping a spoon in 20 to 40 feet of water and pulling up/dropping down is agonizing. Big spoons, at the right time and the right place can produce some nice bass, but it's a lot like work.
- If you're fishing and it's not fun you're doing it wrong.

24

Tales of Ten-Pounders

Once you've landed a true trophy bass, you begin to see things previously unnoticed. The eyes look huge, the simple heft on your hand seems unfamiliar but certainly welcome, the mouth looks gigantic, and the thickness across the back is so much different than the average catch. A five-pounder is an achievement, but once you start landing six, seven, and eight pound bass, your world and perspective changes. Once you catch one BIG bass, next thing it becomes (or at least it did for me) an addiction. My records show more than 300 bass in the seven to nine pound category, and still on very cast I hope for one that challenges me, *stretches my string,* and gets my heart pumping all the way to my lipping this magnificent creature.

I have documented records for over the last 40 years showing catches of well over 1,000 bass weighing more than five pounds, but the most revered number for the bass angler is topping the ten pound mark. Here's the details on my BIG bass tipping the scales at over ten! Keep in mind most of these were caught out of a small aluminum boat or a kayak. This furthers the theory that working small areas that hold BIG fish is critical to catching that fish of a lifetime.

✝✝✝

Your first of anything is always special. It was late December; a

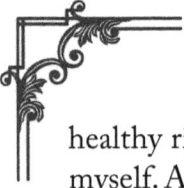

healthy river system was my destination, and I had the water to myself. As I launched, I already had my game plan and three rods rigged with my normal starting artificial lures, one jig rod, one crankbait rod, and a spinnerbait secured to rod number three. Wind and current were pushing me back towards a dam, but my small transom mounted trolling motor kept me fairly steady and as I surveyed the situation, the willowleaf/Colorado combination spinner looked like the best bet to counter the stained water. My target was a long gravel point that fell off into an S-curve in the river. A cast across the downstream side of the point was interrupted in its initial fall, and I set the hook what felt like an unnatural heaviness. The drag slipped, and the tip of the rod met the surface of the water as I reached frantically for the trolling motor handle, and the pull of the fish coupled with the zzz...zzzz... sound of the drag slipping had my blood pumping. What in the world was this? The 50 degree murky water revealed the wide back of the biggest bass I had ever hooked. Another run toward the bottom and with my hands already shaking uncontrollably, I somehow got a firm grip on my first ten-pound bass. I immediately returned to the launch point and placed the bass in a large cooler I carried with me. A close by home kitchen scale read 10 pounds 2 ounces. Wanting to certify my catch I zipped over to the local post office and begged the postmaster to allow the slimy fish to be weighed. Yep, 10 pounds and four ounces of largemouth bass! After two rolls of film the BIG bass was released less than 50 yards from where I caught her on my one and only cast of the day.

Another close to home body of water was the scene of BIG bass number two. Fishing my way to an area that had delivered some solid fish, I had a crawfish pattern jig tied to an old stiff rod that served as a dual-purpose worm rod and jig rod. My first six-pound bass had come from a lake in Missouri on a black jig and pork frog combination on this very rod. It was April, and the fourth month had always been a good month for numbers of bass, and I had hoped to catch at least a dozen fish of any size. Positioned on

a subtle rock drop off that had a line of stumps in about five feet of water I readied myself to cast toward what was my intended target. After a few minutes I made a short cast and then, I sensed what felt like an empty line, like my jig had broken off. It had me looking for where my line entered the water. The line was swimming toward me then took a turn parallel toward the small boat. Making up the slack line quickly, I rocked the boat with my hook set and got what seemed like a counter punch, the next thing I knew a huge bass rocketed through the surface right along side my boat. As I leaned back on this fish, I remember muttering, "Don't get off, don't get off." Two more jumps and the big bass was mine. A slow troll back to my truck, and my fish was secured in a large Styrofoam cooler and taken to a mini-market that I knew had a scale. Running in form the parking lot, I was the object of attention with a BIG bass dripping water all the way into the store. I watched as the scale settled at 10 pounds seven ounces. Questions began, but my only interest was in getting that bass back into the water. That was the day I fell in love with the jig!

There was a small lake that I had gotten access to earlier in the year. Because of the 40-mile drive it wasn't a place that I visited often. A bowl-shaped body of water with a little shoreline cover, it didn't have a big bass look until... It was June. I was working a small spot, and I noticed a bit of water flow and discovered there was a small underwater spring close by a pile of rocks that seemed to deflect the barely noticeable current to either side of the boulders. A Texas rigged worm was at the end of my line, and four straight casts went unrewarded. The next cast slithered across the rocks and moved noticeably to the left, which I attributed to the current push. The bait continued to swim, and I felt a steady strong pressure, and with what could be best described as a defensive hook set, I had hooked a hefty bass. A zig zag path, a jump, a run toward heavy cover, and two more jumps, and that fish was mine. Judging the fish to be another ten-plus trophy, I pushed a small nylon stringer through the lower jaw and tied my prize off to a

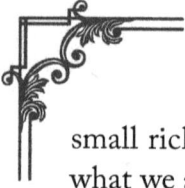

small rickety wooden boat dock nearby. The next few hours are what we as bass anglers dream of, the spring spot kept delivering sizable fish. I would catch one, move off, let it rest, and reload and catch another trophy bass. A hand scale showed my first fish as 10 pounds 8 ounces. Even if the scale was questionable, the fact that this bass broke the ten pound mark was not. That day I had six bass over five pounds with two of them being marked at over seven! Jigs and plastic worms were proving to be BIG bass baits!

†††

While not a ten-pounder there's a special place in my memory and my heart for my biggest smallmouth bass. I had in the past caught several smallies over five pounds. Remote waters, bigger lakes, trolling live bait, throwing a jig, or working a buzzbait over deeper spots had provided smallmouths between five and six and a half, but there was one that stood out above all the others. I was paddling a canoe in Canadian waters, a true wilderness area, a place so special that I visited every year for decades. I had learned a lot about smallmouths even if it was in foreign waters.

For years I had carried a Tupperware bowl of spinnerbaits across the border on my trips into the *Quetico*—three million acres of primitive waters, glacier lakes so pure you could literally drink the water right form the lake. Over several seasons I had learned the a ⅜th ounce double-bladed spinnerbait produced fish after fish, year after year. This was a modified spinner. A smaller Colorado blade in front trailed by a larger Indiana chartreuse blade. The modification was a splash of red spray paint on the back of the big blade and while the paint was still wet, a sprinkle a bit of gold glitter to add some additional flash.

This particular year, late August, the beginning of their fall, the smallmouth were hitting hard enough to frequently knock the blades off the baits! A cast to a steep bluff bank and *BAM*, a sloid hit... and a miss. A quick return got the same reaction, but this time the bass stayed buttoned up. A fight punctuated by five jumps

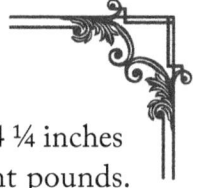

produced a huge potbellied smallmouth that measure 24 ¼ inches long and was later determined to be in excess of eight pounds. Eight, a little less or a little more—that brown bass was a beast!

†††

Where many people shy away from murky water, I often pray for it. Discolored water allows for a close approach which falls into my favorite kind of fishing. Another river system in late November and the deer hunters and the meek of spirit placed me alone on this trip. Downed trees, points, backwaters, and shoreline cover were all a part of the game plan. Anticipating an afternoon bite, I saved my best spots for after 2 PM. A single storm drain was halfway down the bank from my usual places, there was still a thick green weed bed located just below the flow of the drain pipe. From previous experience I had found that muddy water bass would hit a bigger copper colored willowleaf bladed spinnerbait. So far, no fish and then a cast of the modified spinnerbait was absolutely thumped—no question that was a big fish.

A shore line observer noticed the fight, my rod bowed, and I was straining to control the bass. He called out, "That's got to be giant." It was! The tug of war ended as I slid the BIG bass into my grip. My new fan agreed to take a picture for me, and we both marveled at the size of the largemouth bass that had been hiding in ambush below the storm drain. The scale marked this fall fish at an even 10 pounds ten ounces.

In another body if water there was rock-strewn shoreline that lead into a deep drop off and a jungle of big fallen trees. It was a spot I had caught a few decent bass from in the past. I normally go into recollection mode when I reach a place where something memorable has happened, and this was one of those places. I had some big crappie catches and flirted with a few bass catches that were in the four-pound range and even a smallmouth of similar size. All those encounters indicated to me there was a reason fish hovered in that area. Standing and wearing camouflage, as I always

141

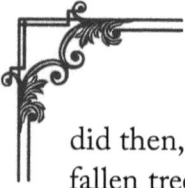

did then, I made a perfect pitch alongside the trunk of a massive fallen tree. The jig barely dimpled the surface, and its swim back toward me was interrupted by a solid thump. My fishing partner was stunned by the sight of a huge largemouth jumping almost in front of him and blurted out, "Do you want me to get the camera?" To which I replied, "Forget the camera; get the net!"

This was a potbellied prespawn bass that looked like it was ready to bust. I worked the monster bass back alongside the flat bottom boat and then back to the waiting net. Let the celebration begin. This one brought the scale to rest at 10 pounds 11 ounces!

I never had a fascination for *frog fishing*. I had seen and heard others rave about throwing a soft surface frog imitator among the thick grass, moss, aquatic weeds, and lily pads, but always thought of presenting different bass baits, like my beloved buzzbait, in those places. It was mid-August, and I was in a place I had previously fished and was intrigued by the never-ending patches of lily pads. In anticipation of throwing the leopard pattern frog into the dense field of dollar pads, the smaller version of this aquatic vegetation, I surveyed the situation still not sold on the froggy. A few casts, a slower cadence, and then a blow up, a swing, and a miss. A few more top water explosions and no hook up sent me thinking of other approaches that might pull fish from the pads.

Silently I thought, *One more try,* then I eyeballed a promising spot and... *bam,* a three-ponder came in wearing a disguise of lily pads and stems. Fueled by that success, I paddled my kayak into a massive section of the pads. Bluegill were actively feeding on dragonflies, and I watched as big swirls appeared to be chasing the bluegill. A cast deep into the maze of dollar pads, hop, twitch, rest, hop, twitch, *BOOM!* The hook set encased bass and a wad of the greenery, but the fish had a mighty pull. Fearing the loss of what felt like a giant, I maneuvered toward the combination of bass and pads all the while keeping a steady pressure on the fish. I scooped up fish, weeds and water and flopped them into the bottom of the kayak. A ten-pound frog fish lay at my feet.

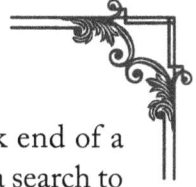

Another heavyweight came from a cove in the back end of a lake that was new to me. I was running a spinnerbait as a search to find cover and possibly a fish. In the middle of the area was what felt like a single stump. I love single secondary objects because if there's a bass anywhere near the area, often they will gravitate to just such a place. Also because of the noticeable depth change indicating a creek channel as well as the presence of the stump, I moved closer and made the decision to pick up the jig rod. Even the laziest bass will eat if there's a free meal swimming close enough by them. First cast, and I felt the bait bump the stump. Cast number two was followed by a pronounced jig type thump. I set the hook with a vengeance, and the response was a heavy pull followed by a series of jumps from a truly BIG bass. I reached behind me to grab my net as I worked the fish toward me, and the bass plunged under my kayak, I abandon the idea of the net with the plan to lip this monster. With the trophy boat side I grabbed and *missed,* which seemed to make this fish fight harder and dive deeper. I went back to the net plan and fought the bass back to within inches and was able to get her into the net. She later scaled at 10 pounds two ounces.

It was April 4th, 2015—the moon phase was full, and I couldn't wait to get to one of my best spots to look for a *lunker.* A recent rain had the river moving with a small current, while the water showed a stain that would help to hide my presence from the fish. Typically, in current, I paddle the kayak up stream and use the current to propel me and employ the paddle to position me. I passed a bank full of fallen trees and slid into a small flat that had a point with a few stumps on it. That area looked promising, so I paddled back upstream to make another pass. No bites, so I angled toward a small but solid well-defined point with an overhanging tree. I liked this spot because if there was any flow it delivered food sources to the fish, and usually one side or the other of the point had a fish on it, I describe such places as a *one fish spot.* With an underhand pendulum swing I sent a jig to the base of the tree, the bait made

a silent entry, and almost immediately I watched as the line swam quartering away, very noticeably because it was against the current. My line passed the point and swam by within inches of my boat. The bite wasn't a surprise, but the fish at the end surely was. As big a bass as I had ever seen was ready to rumble. I was amazed by the thickness of this fish; it was unlike any had hooked before. I was standing to cast, but as is my habit, I sit down to fight bigger bass. Often the bigger bass head to cover or deep water when hooked, and this one was wasting no time headed deep. I turned her toward me praying the hook set was good and the knot was tight enough to hold. Each time she turned I countered by turning her in the opposite direction hoping to wear her down quickly. After what was probably 45 seconds but seemed like an hour, I slid my thumb firmly into the jaw of my biggest bass ever, 11 pounds 3 ounces!

These along with other truly BIG bass are etched in my memory forever.

25

Targeting Trophies

These are the concepts I use every time out. I've communicated these messages on TV, doing radio, in print magazines, in newspaper, and blogging. I've added to them over the years but rarely eliminated any. This is the map to follow to your biggest bass ever!

- **Depth**—Center your search in waters three to eight feet deep. You'll find bass shallower or deeper, but I have consistently find the BIG bass in and around this depth.
- **Moon Phase**—The current world record bass, 22' 4" caught by George Perry, was caught a few days before a full moon. Checking data from several record fish both fresh and salt water proves the theory that the moon phase full or new has a powerful influence on record class fish.
- **Retrieve Speed**—Your retrieve speed determines in large part the reaction of the bass. Too fast and they ignore the lure, slow (on the *feel* type baits) is almost always better
- **Random Action**—This factor is why bass never get wise to lures that posses this quality. Generally silent, easy to swallow, natural colors, a realistic swimming motion, and the random action inherent in the bait and supplied by each differently bass angler.
- **Resistance**—Recognizing the hit, pick up, bite, or whatever term you like, in feel bait fishing it's vital to concentrate all

the time, recognize anything that feels *different,* and when in doubt SET THE HOOK. Always believe the next cast could be the biggest bass of your life. One day it will be.

- **Up Close And Personal**—I prefer to be in close proximity to the fish. Shorter casts mean less line out and the potential for a solid hook set and getting the bass in quickly. Rarely do I flip, but 90% of my feel bait fishing is close range pitching. The longer you fight a fish the more likely it is to get off. Get them in quickly. That's what the heavy tackle is designed for.
- **Make The Bait Look Alive**—Many baits have a built-in action; most rely on the angler to seal the deal. Understanding what the real thing looks like, its natural motion, and speed is vital. Observation of the food sources is time well spent—the look, the movements, and every detail.
- **Strike Zone**—The strike zone has become exaggerated by media accounts and fish tales. A BIG bass will minimize its movement to feed; that's how they get big and stay big. The shorter the distance a BIG bass has to move, the more likely the bite. Silent and stealthy are invaluable.
- **Four Needs**—Find an area that serves all the needs of a BIG bass, and it will stay until something changes. Oxygen, food, cover, and deep water. If the food source dries up, the water drops dramatically, or if oxygen is depleted by high heat, they will form a home area, learn it, and stay in it. If a BIG bass is caught out, moved, or dies another will take up residence in that spot.
- **Play To Your Strengths/The Weakness Of The Fish**—If you're an expert at spinnerbaits, throw it; cranking, crank it. Use you best technique and understand where fish are, why they're there, and what they will do under most circumstances. It's like an underwater chess game. Experience is the best teacher. And expand your knowledge and confidence in other baits and techniques.
- **Learn Three Knots**—For 90% of what you'll do you need

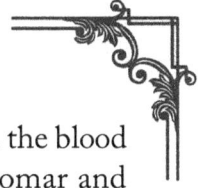

to learn three knots—the Palomar, the clinch, and the blood knot to tie leaders. With braided line tie a Palomar and follow it up with a clinch knot to avoid the braid slipping. If you're unsatisfied with your knot or line, RETIE! Heat is the enemy of most lines but for sure monofilament. Wet your knots before cinching down.

- **Mental Preparation**—Deer hunters call it *buck fever*—the big buck shows up, and they're mentally unprepared. BIG bass can cause the same illness. I never make a cast that I don't believe I'm not going to catch a fish; true story! Be ready, have a plan, minimize mistakes. BIG bass are unforgiving. Strong line, a good knot, correctly set drag, and letting the rod do its job are all essential to catching BIG bass regularly.

- **Find And Fish Big Bass Waters**—Not ever body of water is a BIG fish factory. Look for places with a reputation for BIG bass, pictures of BIG bass, tales told by old timers about BIG bass catches. Investigate the water quality and available food sources.

- **Tackle the Issue of Tackle**—Gear up for the BIG bass battle. This is no time for cheap, old, worn-out equipment. Better to have a few top quality (not necessarily expensive) rod and reel combos, keep reels lubricated and fresh line spooled, give constant attention to hooks being "Sticky" sharp—it all pays off when your BIG bass is on the line. Take care of your tackle.

- **Watch for Natural Signs**—Gulls and herons feeding are an indication of the presence of bait fish. Watch wind direction; north is cooling, south is warming. In cooler or colder weather you're more likely to get an afternoon bite. Shorter days and cooler nights signal to fish that winter is approaching; be ready for feeding binges. Walk and watch the shorelines for minnow hatches, bugs, crawfish, and frogs; all of these are indications of varied food sources and poten-tial artificial bait choices.

- **Learn to Fish the "Feel" Baits**—BIG bass are caught on every category of artificial lure but to tilt the odds in your favor for a giant learn to fish jigs, plastic worms, and other soft plastic baits. Concentrate, constant contact and set the hook on anything that feels different. Try to improve your approach each year with a different bait or technique. When in doubt throw the jig/worm.

- **Vertical Versus Horizontal**—Fish of any kind are in a neutral or negative most of the time. Bass, especially BIG ones, are opportunistic feeders, food happens by… food gets eaten. Fish in a negative/neutral feeding mode can often be caught using a vertical presentation (this is why flipping works), aggressively feeding fish will chase (for a short distance *see Strike Zone) horizontally presented baits. Couple both approaches with the correct speed, and you'll get bit.

- **No Sight NO Bite**—The primary sense for feeding and survival in a bass is sight. The other senses under normal conditions are a distant second. Hearing generally is more associated with negatives responses. Smell is almost of zero importance. Taste, the bass already has it in it's mouth so...set the hook! Watch what your bait looks like on the presentation.

- **Looking for a Lunker Largemouth**—Get off the bank and seek out secondary cover. Pressured fish and falling water will send bass of all sizes to secondary cover. If they want to visit the bank, it's a short trip; if they want to go deeper, it's a short trip. Put that cover on three to eight feet of water, and you're in BIG bass country.

- **Smallmouth Search**—Start deep and then go deeper. Find the crawfish and shad. Swim a grub or other soft plastic. If your heart is strong enough, throw top water baits in the spring and fall. Smallmouths are tough to pattern, ignore shallow water and objects, think deep.

- **Common Senses**—Electronics or not, learn to read the

water, follow your instincts. Observation, experience, and intuitive clues will take you to BIG bass. Electronics in conjunction with common sense and experience make you hard to beat. What would you do if your batteries failed? What if you're fishing for food in a survival situation? Tap into your intuitive skills. Trust your gut.

- **Tackle Trade Off**—Downsize your tackle box to lures that you can count on. Carry spares of the best ones; keep best producers of the soft plastics handy in your pocket. Change to seasonal tackle choices based off weather and water conditions. Be honest; you already know what you're going to throw. I retie baits more than I ever change baits.

- **Cast Away**—Cast past where you believe your bass is positioned, their field of vision is pretty wide, but the less time it has to make up it's mind on *food or fake* the better chance you have. Learn to cast as quietly as possible, and let the lures do what they are designed to do.

- **Small/Slow**—If fishing is tough, try smaller lures and slower retrieves. This will generally produce a few bites, not big bass, but enough to keep you interested and maybe a renegade bigger bass looking for an easy meal. I've caught some big fish using this method.

- **One Size Fits All**—Not 100% true, but I rely on ⅜th ounce fixed weighted baits (jigs, spinners, buzzers, Texas rigs) most of the time. Reason: they feel the same when casting and retrieving, at least for me. I learned to develop a feel on the retrieve, and this becomes similar to a muscle memory. For me, to keep my casts deadly accurate, picking up the same weight bait constantly helps.

- **Alterations**—Because we all fish in spots that probably get a fair amount of fishing pressure, the bass are repeatedly getting exposed to the same or similar baits, and since they feed mostly by sight I change the lures in some way to give them a different visual appeal. Blade changes on spinnerbaits,

149

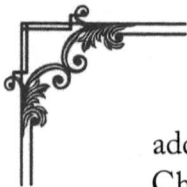

add, remove, or apply painted blades to your favorite spinner. Changing out front trebles on cranking baits to a red treble adds a brief glimpse of red for the predatory bass. The addition of a small willow leaf blade to the rear of my buzzbait has really helped. There are several ways to alter your lures... try something different.

These concepts have helped me for decades; add a few, mark out a few, keep throwing—the biggest bass of your life could be on the next cast.

Big Bass Magic

A Once In A Lifetime Spot

Imagine a fishing hole that you discovered almost accidentally, close to home, accessible, and full of fish—giant fish. This place would be magical, diverse, clean, and have nothing but wild fish. Think of this place as a virgin fishery, managed naturally, it received minimal pressure and that was by people of limited resources and skills. This dream spot was seemingly to be untouched by the human hand and have an assortment of cover and conditions and promised unbelievable catches for decades. Does this sound mythical? I found a place like this. It looked like many spots I had seen before but gave no clue to the future it offered below the surface. It was bordered by country roads, history, and fertile farm land. It's secrets and stories would be revealed slowly. Unintentional success came as unexpectedly as the days, weeks, months, and years drifted by like its current. Changes to the area, the banks, and life forms occurred organically, tragically, and sometimes drastically, but always my mistress bounced back.

At times the river water was more like my life blood flowing through my veins; it saw me through many difficult times. I went there to confess my sins, to celebrate my life, and to find my balance. The river never lied to me, was always available, kept all its promises, and comforted me during hard times. In return I protected her secrets, worked to keep her clean, and honored her. Not to be outdone, she delivered big fish and big memories. I spent days

151

learning all I could about her and her "friends." I was introduced to foxes, beavers, muskrats, osprey, several types of snakes, herons, owls, coyotes, deer, quail, turkeys, ducks, geese, and yes multiple species of fish—oh the fish!

At first, they came as surprise. What?! A crappie in this fishing hole? Then came a few bluegill, and eventually a bass, a good one, probably 2 ½ pounds. I could have never imagined how this place would change my life and the lessons I would learn in the most basic boats and through every season.

My river reflections include invasions by people, progress, and lack of respect for the resource. I foolishly thought, maybe hoped, it would always be sustainable and maintained by the gatekeepers who would learn to love her to like I did. I saw the dark side of the river as it claimed lives of those who challenged it and disrespected its power. I watched helplessly as it was abused in every possible way, even as I worked to maintain it.

Often I recall in private moments my introduction to it. An older gentleman sitting on the banks, who always built a small fire, sat on one bucket and had one close by to hold his catch. I recall seeing other people bringing their kids to the shoreline with a blue bait cup full of worms and the excitement for the possibilities of a catch. Large numbers of fair-weather fishermen in the spring, numbers that dwindled in the summer and many were non-existent in the fall and winter. Few recognizable faces consistently visited and none who worshipped the river like I did. All along I wondered how long this love affair would last. I agonized over seeing people pulling stringers of fish out of the water. I tried not to think about that or people who were raping *my* river. Trash, over-harvest, abuse of the resource—it was too painful to watch. There were occasional reminders of how the river could heal itself; a giant autumn fish, proof that this one made it through the season and might spawn again. Countless hours were spent learning the lessons that were given up begrudgingly by the river.

This place became a living laboratory. The definition of scientific

experiment contains these elements; observation, asking questions, forming a hypothesis, making a prediction, testing and forming a hypothesis based off results. I had a certain degree of control over my environment, I was looking (fishing) for repeatable results and then coming to a conclusion from the measured results. In plain language, I could fish a specific spot, using techniques that I understood, and then log results to determine what and how fish reacted to every aspect of my approach. Sounds dry, right? Now imagine pitching jigs to fish that had never seen one, further consider the places were small but full of cover, food sources, and the environment was ideal for producing quality fish, kind of a fishing heaven.

When I studied weather and water conditions, catches became more predictable. Each different access spot on the river offered a microcosm of any water almost anywhere. There were many forms of aquatic vegetation, tree lined shore and submerged stumps and fallen trees, creek channels, bottom contours, a few manmade boats slips, docks, points, gravel bars, chunk rock, bridge pilings, secondary creeks entering, and current. The balance of fish was ideal, all three major species of bass, largemouth, smallmouth and the spotted Kentucky bass, bluegill, flathead catfish, carp, red eye and crappie also inhabited this place.

The introduction of new lures and techniques was exciting—so exciting often times I couldn't sleep the night before in anticipation of the fish that would be fooled by something they had never seen before. There were several locations and access points that were simple and some that required my turtle imitation, namely hauling a green boat on my back a quarter of a mile in order to slide it into my secret spot. My means of propulsion was a marine battery and a trolling motor. It was an adventure casting a jig into waters teeming with big bass that had not seen this swimming, hopping, darting crawfish imitating creature before; they couldn't wait to *taste* it.

If you were willing to do the work to reach spots for a rough,

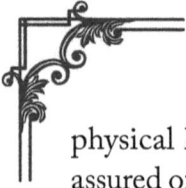

physical launch you could sling a buzzbait around cover and be assured of at least one five-pound bass. Oh, there were a few people who would make their way in, but they tried to force the fish to take the standard minnow rig, or tight line a live red wiggler worm, but they soon tired of the game. People had minimal success when they began to try to imitate what they saw me doing. The word spread about this guy catching big fish in this unlikely looking place. I foolishly sought notoriety for my catches and sent photos to the local newspaper and to the *bragging boards* of sporting goods stores and TV stations. This made it difficult to remain anonymous around a small town loaded with outdoorsmen.

The more I learned, the more I became obsessed with the river and the fish. Five pound bass became common; rarely did I even test myself against the other species—this bass mecca was intoxicating. With the heavy hits I was getting, a five pounder was almost anticlimactic, a disappointment. The smallmouth began to disappear due to the loss of habitat, slow moving waters, and the increase in water temperatures. Their spawning and lifestyle weren't really suited to these changes. The *spots* were a nuisance, even though they put on an aerial display after being hooked. Largemouth bass from six to eight pounds started to show up regularly. Then a few nine-pound bass were added to my journal of catches. Ten pounds and four ounces, a new personal best bass. Seven times in my life I would top ten pounds—three in this magic place—a seven-pound smallmouth, a four-pound spotted, and a crappie 19 ½ inches that would weigh in at just over four pounds all came from the secret river waters.

It would be impossible to place a value on the lessons I learned in thirty years fishing this incredible place. What I learned translated to being able to duplicate my success all across North America. I transcribed my thoughts to the pages of magazines, made outline notes to use doing seminars, prepared radio scripts to instruct others, and occasionally brought TV cameras to my honey hole while insisting no shoreline shots were allowed that might reveal

our location. Fish behavior, seasonal migration, life style, feeding preferences, and predictable location all became second nature to me.

I watched as farm fields gave way to parking lots and apartments. Word of upstream chemical spills would create panic until I could check the impact of the interruption. There was no question the river was paying the price for progress—they were raping my river. In time I'll tell of the eventual fate of the river. But that is a story for another time.

I haven't been back to that place for almost two years. I'm afraid. I'm afraid to go back because I fear the place I came to love will no longer love me back or be the same; that I'll be...disappointed.

Is it possible that the progeny of the fish I released will reward me with a big bite? Will it spoil the memories I have of a safe haven, a place that shaped and saved my life?

Oh, in time I'll go back, face my fear, and maybe realize the memories can't be tarnished by a poor day fishing, or a less than perfect experience.

But will the magic still be there?

We'll have to wait and see.

My Go-To Baits

These are the exact baits I use most regularly, there some are for other species, still others are no longer manufactured but have proven to be effective for catching trophy fish. These are BIG bass baits!

- **Jigs**—My #1 BIG bass bait. ⅜th ounce Strike King Denny Brauer structure jig, equipped with an Owner hook and the three colors I use most often are #101 Bama craw, #18 Watermelon red flake and #2 Black/blue. The Hack Attack Flipping Jig again ⅜th ounce in colors #8 Texas craw, #50 Okeechobee craw. For cold water applications the Strike King Tour Grade Football Jig ⅜th ounce #18 Watermelon red #50 Okeechobee craw and #100 Summer craw.
- **Soft Plastic for Jig Trailers or Texas Rigs**—Rage Tail Craw #18 Watermelon red flake, #46 Green Pumpkin, #101 Bama Craw, #229 Roadkill Baby Rage Tail baby craw SAME COLORS.
- **Soft Plastic Worms Texas and Wacky Rig**—I've caught several bass over six pounds on the 7 inch Rage Tail Anaconda. Best color for me was Okeechobee Craw (discontinued), #18 Watermelon red flake #46 Green Pumpkin 7 inch Cut-R-Worm #50 Okeechobee craw, #466 Crawdaddy
- **Tubes**—Denny Brauer Flip-N-Tube 4.5 #2 Black Blue

157

Flake, #38 Black Neon, #46 Green Pumpkin, Wacky rig Strike King Zero #18 Watermelon red flake, #101 Bama Craw

- **Buzzbaits**—Bass Specialties (no longer in business) ⅜th ounce large buzz blade with a willow leaf blade attached to the back of the arm. Double Trouble, Springer baits (No longer on business) ¼ ounce two small blades side by side for slower retrieve and less noise and top water disturbance.
- **Surface Frogs**—Strike King KVD Sexy Frog, Leopard Frog, Green Pumpkin/Pearl Belly and Black.
- **Crankbaits**—1.5 Squarebill Strike King colors #517 Tennessee Shad, #535 Black back chartreuse #584 Oyster #667 DB Craw #699 Natural Shad. Lipless Crankbaits Strike King Red Eye Shad ½ ounce AND ¼ ounce #408 Chrome Blue, #451 Rayburn Red (muddy water) #584 Oyster Berkley Rattl-R Threadfin Shad pattern (discontinued) Storm Wiggle Wart, Bone color, Brown Crawdad and Hot Tiger. Medium Diver Poe's (no longer in business) made of cedar #200 and #300 Spook pattern.
- **Minnow Imitator**—A.C. Shiner #300 C shad pattern, silver/black back. #375 same colors
- **Spinnerbait**—Strike King ⅜th ounce Willow/Colorado combination (gold willow/nickel Colorado) ⅜th ounce double willow (muddy water) Bass Pro Shops Tornado (no longer available)

All around baits for bass, crappie, and more, I have caught BIG bass on each.

- **Charlie Brewer Slider Four Inch Slider**—worm colors, tomato, purple, motor oil and black. Three inch bass grub in Pearl/chartreuse tail, Pearl, Purple/chartreuse tail and Tennessee Shad
- **MidSouth Tackle**—tubes 0095 Monteleone Silver, 0650

Bloodshot, 0100 GL pearl glow, 820 C chartreuse red flake. ⅛th ounce Sickle leadhead

- **RODS/REELS**—The majority of what I use are Lew's Rods and Reels. Because of the various uses, different techniques I recommend you go to their website for more information. My jig/worm set up is a Lew's Magnum Bass model LCLMBR 7' 0" Medium/Heavy action with a fast tip. My reel is the Lew's Tournament light TLT1SH that weighs 5.8 ounces, has a 7.5:1 retrieve ratio pulling 31 inches of line on each handle revolution. This is my work horse.

- **My Lines**—K9 (K9fishing.com) for braid 25/40 lb. test and fluorocarbon. For monofilament Sufix 12 lb. test

Acknowledgements

The purpose of this book is twofold: to credit those who have assisted me in my pursuit if trophy bass and to assist others in the same quest. My goal is for the lessons I've learned to live on and have others feel the same exhilaration I have hundreds of times in landing genuine trophy bass. Every catch should be celebrated, but the successful catch of a BIG bass is surely something special. A kid fishing a creek with a cane pole, the tournament pro, and everyone in between should know the feeling of fooling the superior of the species.

To my Heavenly Father: my thanks for the skills you have bestowed upon me, for taking me to magical places, all the while protecting me and teaching me. Thanks for bringing people into my life that have made me a better person, for clear vision to see your creations, for opportunities on and off the water, protecting me, and for being the Ultimate Guide.

To my Earthly Father; thanks for passing on the blueprint for living the American Dream. Hard work, dedication, and persistence pays off.

To my mentors and friends who have come before me and in some cases left just the lessons, memories, and words indelibly engrained in my mind. This volume is dedicated to Bill Dance who made me smile, called me friend, and for decades showed us all how to catch fish while being better humans. To Doug Hannon;

who taught me more about giant bass in a few years than I could have learned in a lifetime on my own. I'm passing it on, Doug. To Homer Circle; who believed in me when few others did, who advised me and taught me about the *bass business*. To people in and out of the outdoor industry, people who guided me, trusted me, gave me a place to fish and a platform to communicate my message. People like Steve Parks, Tommy Akin, Jimmy Yates, Garry Mason, Brenda Valentine, Earl Bentz, Dave Precht, Bill Cody, Charlie Mattos, Don King, Vance Zahorski—to all who supported this wild, crazy notion that I could be an outdoor writer, radio and TV personality, seminar speaker, and fishing guide.

To Michael Vines who patiently watched, encouraged, and guided me through the process of becoming a book author.

To those who have a special place in my heart as fishing friends; friends who turned into family. Met by chance, friends by choice: Tom Braig, Tony Evans, Nathan and Sherry Burnett, Bill Taylor, Bill Herzer, Barry Hackett, Nick Weaver, Bill Hall, Brian Hercules, Chris Nischan, Ian Rahal, and Glen Brian.

To my wife, Debbie, who has mastered bass fishing and braves the wind, rain, heat, and cold in the search for her first ten-pounder. She loves God, family, me, and fishing.

Special thanks to our German Shepherd, Samurai, who for over twelve years has been our protector and pal, truly a member of the family of whom we requested often, "Watch the house, Sami, we're going fishing."

To all those who are inspired by the belief that the next cast could fool the BIGGET bass of your life, this book is the road map to that achievement. Keep casting, hoping, and daring to dream about that one that DOESN'T get away.

About The Author

Joey Monteleone has spent decades in the pursuit of trophy bass. Joey's work includes multimedia communicator in print on the pages of major magazines, newspapers, and blog posts. On radio he served as the outdoor editor for AM 650 WSM on the long running *Wild Side Radio Show*. For more than 35 years he was a TV personality, popular seminar speaker, and in-demand guest on podcasts. His awards included being inducted into the Legends of the Outdoors Hall of Fame, and most recently being honored as the 2024 Communicator of the Year by the Tennessee Wildlife Federation, a national award for community service, and several other achievements. He's landed (and documented) more than 50,000 bass in the last 40 years with more 1,500 weighing in at over five pounds, with an eight-pound smallmouth, seven largemouth bass over 10 pounds, and another over 11 pounds to his credit.

Joey is the author of three books on fishing, has spent years guiding trophy bass fishing trips, is a three-time Eastern United States fishing champion, and holds a third degree black belt in Wado Ryu karate. He's spent much of his adult life studying bass, learning their secrets and perfecting his presentation skills to consistently catch giants.

Joey lives with his wife, Debbie, in Decherd, Tennessee, on the banks of Woods Reservoir.

You can contact Joey at fishjoey10@gmail.com

Also from WordCrafts Press

In the Company of Dogs
by Dr. Jeannette Barnes, DVM

Never Run a Dead Kata
by Rodney Lewis Boyd

The Scoutmaster
by Brooks Eason

When the Other Boot Drops
by Jeff Keene II

www.WordCrafts.net